IMPERIAL
WAR
MUSEUMS

Published in 2020 by Welbeck

An imprint of Welbeck Non-Fiction Limited,
Part of Welbeck Publishing Group
20 Mortimer Street
London W1T 3JW

A CIP catalogue record for this book is available from the British Library

ISBN 978-1-78739-490-2

Project Editor: Chris Mitchell
Project Designer: Darren Jordan
Production: Marion Storz

10 9 8 7 6 5 4 3 2 1

Printed in Great Britain

The publishers would like to thank the following sources for their kind permission to reproduce the pictures in this book.

Page 13: Bettmann/Getty Images. 59: Shutterstock. 93: (top left) www.loc.gov/item/96523441; (top centre) IWM D 1966; (top right) IWM HU 10180; (bottom left) IWM FLM 1506; (bottom centre) Wikimedia commons; (bottom right) IWM HU 90973.

PICTURE QUIZ

Page 1: (top) IWM Q 80362; (bottom left) IWM Q 6298; (bottom right) IWM Q 11685. 2: (top) IWM Q 14479; (centre) IWM Q 49249; (bottom) IWM Q 14638. 3: (top) IWM Q 64476; (centre) IWM Q 64483; (bottom) IWM Q 14492. 4: (left) ullstein bild Dtl./Getty Images; (right) IWM Q 13560. 5: (top) Wikimedia commons; (bottom) IWM Q 68033. 6: IWM Q 11428. 7: (top left) Granger/Shutterstock; (top right) Shutterstock; (bottom) IWM Q 11878. 8: (top) IWM PST 11007; (bottom) IWM Q 21382. 9: (top) IWM Q 43227; (centre) IWM Q 21661A; (bottom) IWM Q 75282. 10: (top) IWM MH 13110; (bottom) IWM HU 47654. 11: (top) Wikimedia commons; (bottom) IWM HU 55635. 12: (top) IWM E 3900E; (bottom) IWM FRE 8857. 13: (top) IWM C 5423; (centre) IWM EMOS 1380; (bottom) IWM CM 4954. 14: (left) IWM A 20794; (right) IWM TR 1039. 15: (top left) IWM CH 13020; (top right) IWM D 26065; (bottom left) IWM D 1417; (bottom right) IWM A 9760. 17: (top left) Wikimedia commons/UK Public Record Office; (top right) IWM COM 921A; (centre left) IWM A 23510; (centre right) ZUMA Press, Inc./Alamy Stock Photo; (bottom left) Wikimedia commons. 18: (top) IWM HU 374; (bottom) IWM FL 1472. 19: (top) IWM Q 14055; (centre) IWM Q 58246; (bottom) IWM MH 6177. 20: (top) IWM A 4154; (bottom) IWM EA 51048. 21: (top) IWM HU 68178; (centre) IWM HU 89821; (bottom) IWM HU 1755. 22: (top) NASA; (bottom) Wikimedia commons/The John F. Kennedy Presidential Library and Museum, Boston. 23: (top) NASA; (bottom) IWM CT 1494. 24: (top) www.loc.gov/item/2003662344; (bottom) AP/Shutterstock. 25: (top) Everett Collection/Shutterstock; (bottom left) Tim Rooke/Shutterstock; (bottom right) Laski Diffusion/Getty Images. 26: (top) IWM CT 154; (bottom) Wikimedia commons. 27: (top) Leonid Yakutin/AP/Shutterstock; (centre) AP/Shutterstock; (bottom) IWM BF 399. 28: (top) David Fowler/Shutterstock; (bottom) Wikimedia Commons/RIA Novosti. 29: (top) www.loc.gov/item/2018651363; (centre left) www.loc.gov/item/2019646345; (centre right) www.loc.gov/item/96522672; (bottom) www.loc.gov/item/2011633940.

IMPERIAL WAR MUSEUMS

OVER 100 PUZZLES AND ENIGMAS

CAN YOU CRACK THE WARTIME CODES?

RICHARD GALLAND

CONTENTS

ABOUT IMPERIAL WAR MUSEUMS

Imperial War Museums (IWM) is a family of five museums and the world's leading authority on conflict and its impact on people's lives. Founded in the midst of the First World War, with a mission to preserve and tell the stories of all kinds of people from around the world, it continues to do this work right up to present-day conflict.

IWM collects objects and stories that give an insight into people's experiences of war, preserving them for future generations, and bringing them to today's audience in the most powerful way possible. As well as their permanent displays, IWM has a dynamic programme of temporary exhibitions, events and educational activities. Their programmes help visitors get close to the lives of those affected by war and develop a deeper understanding of its effect on the world.

THE ART OF SECRET COMMUNICATION

The practice of concealing information is as old as humanity. Aspiring rulers and warlords throughout history have depended on their carefully laid plans not falling into the wrong hands. In fact, some of the techniques used to create secret messages millennia ago have been so effective that they continued to be employed – with increasing sophistication – up to and including the Second World War.

Today, secret communication is no longer the preserve of kings and generals. We all value our privacy, and our emails and text messages are encrypted by systems too complex for even the greatest human minds to untangle without electronic help.

Imagine you have travelled back in time to an era before electronic communications. You are a general at war, and you need to send an important message to one of your allies in a faraway land. The message could mean the difference between victory and defeat. If the enemy were to intercept and read the message, however, all would be lost. What do you do?

CONCEAL YOUR MESSAGE WITH STEGANOGRAPHY

It goes without saying that you should avoid drawing attention to the messenger. But what about the message itself? You might conceal it inside something that the enemy would not consider suspicious, such as an item of clothing, a work of art or even another message.

The practice of hiding a message within non-secret text or data is called steganography (which means 'covered writing'). Here are a few examples:

TATTOOS

An early form of steganography involved shaving a messenger's head, having the message tattooed onto their scalp, and then waiting for the hair to grow back! They would need another trip to the barber at their destination so that the message could be read. Life must have been considerably slower in the ancient world!

INVISIBLE INK

There are many liquids, from lemon juice to urine, that turn almost clear when written on parchment but become visible when exposed to heat or light. A message in secret ink would often be written between the lines of a regular message. Secret inks were first used over 2,000 years ago but were also employed as recently as during the Second World War. Today, a similar effect can be achieved with UV ink, although it is considered more suitable for household security than espionage.

MICRODOTS

Photographic shrinkage using microfilm was pioneered in the nineteenth century by the French inventor René Dagron. During the Franco-Prussian War, Paris was under siege. Dagron proposed sending miniaturized messages in and out of the city, and across the Prussian lines, with carrier pigeons. An entire newspaper page could be shrunk onto a tiny roll of film, small enough to be attached to a bird's leg. By the time of the First World War, the technique had been refined further, and it was possible to shrink a message to the size of a full stop.

PUZZLE 1

What symbol should replace the question mark?

Clue: Contemplate

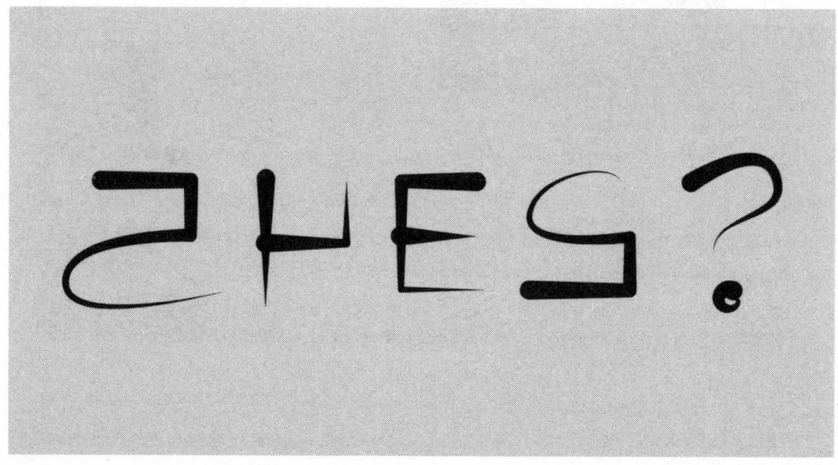

✎ ....

PUZZLE 2

Can you complete this cryptography-themed crossword? If you are struggling with some of the answers, reading the rest of this chapter might help.

ACROSS

4 Computer used by British codebreakers during the Second World War (8)
7 Binary digit (3)
8 Roman who gave his name to a letter-shift code (6)
11 One who leaks codes, most likely (7)
14 Italian architect who gave his name to a polyalphabetic code (7)
15 5 down, perhaps (5)
16 'Word' of binary digits (4)
17 British intelligence and security organization (inits) (4)

DOWN

1 Code that uses a matrix of 25 letters (8)
2 Former code-breaking machine at Bletchley Park (5)
3 Modern 'is this a human' online entry test (7)
4 Code (6)
5 One who searches for secrets (3)
6 It tells computers what to do (8)
9 Code invented by Vigenère (7)
10 Type of error-correcting code; representable by a straight line, mathematically (6)
11 He played a key role in cracking Second World War codes (6)
12 Code originally used in Hebrew (6)
13 It's all dots and dashes (5)

SOLUTIONS PAGE 176

NULL CIPHER

Not all steganography techniques require tools to conceal and reveal their messages. The null cipher hides messages in plain sight within other sentences. For example, this text has a conveniently implanted clue and a secret message:

Although it seems a pointless exercise, this little clue might be relevant: first from each of the third. However, it might not be evident at first. Sometimes we only see what we assume to be germane, missing the essential.

If you only read the first letter of every third word, it reveals:

SECRET MESSAGE.

PUZZLE 3

You are trying to locate your enemy's secret rendezvous in London and have intercepted the following scrap of highly dubious prose. When and where are they meeting?

The afternoon was hot but those mad dogs, all sweaty and tanned, were still loitering outside. They preened like kings while I grew cross and quite exasperated. Oh, it would be nigh on impossible to know what they came for.

MORSE, OF COURSE

Morse code, which consists of letters made up of short 'dots' and long 'dashes', also has a variety of uses in steganography. Each letter, for example, can be knitted into fabric and worn by a messenger.

In 1966, almost a year after he was shot down and captured by North Vietnamese forces, Commander Jeremiah Denton Jr. of the United States Navy was forced to film a propaganda interview that was later broadcast in Japan and the USA. To convey to the world that he was being mistreated by his captors, Commander Denton blinked a message to the cameras in Morse code:

TORTURE.

INTERNATIONAL MORSE CODE ALPHABET

A	•▬	H	••••	O	▬▬▬	V	•••▬
B	▬•••	I	••	P	•▬▬•	W	•▬▬
C	▬•▬•	J	•▬▬▬	Q	▬▬•▬	X	▬••▬
D	▬••	K	▬•▬	R	•▬•	Y	▬•▬▬
E	•	L	•▬••	S	•••	Z	▬▬••
F	••▬•	M	▬▬	T	▬		
G	▬▬•	N	▬•	U	••▬		

PUZZLE 4

Each letter of the alphabet has been encrypted to a number (1 to 26). Crack the code to solve the puzzle and reveal the long cryptographic word hidden somewhere within the grid. To start you off, the codes for three letters have been given.

A	25	24	13	8	■	1	2	20	13	7	17	13	25	N
B	■	13	■	13	■	2	■	26	■	1	■	19	■	O
C	13	6	26	18	17	13	■	16	18	11	9	13	16 M	P
D	■	26	■	24	■	11	■	12	■	12	■	■	■	Q
E	22	13	16	3	■	22	17	3	16	26	4	26	22	R
F	■	22	■	14	■	■	■	14	■	■	■	14	■	S
G	22	17	13	21	18	14	1	21	24	18	12	9	11	T
H	■	13	■	■	■	13	■	■	■	12	■	13	■	U
I	18	25	19	1	7	18	17	13	■	1	3	4	11	V
J	■	■	■	15	■	24	■	22	■	4	■	12 P	■	W
K	13	14	24 R	1	2	13	■	22	7	1	10	10	22	X
L	■	3	■	14	■	22	■	18	■	21	■	26	■	Y
M	13	23	12	13	24	17	4	11	■	11	1	4	5	Z

1	2	3	4	5	6	7	8	9	10	11	12	13
											P	
14	**15**	**16**	**17**	**18**	**19**	**20**	**21**	**22**	**23**	**24**	**25**	**26**
		M								R		

SOLUTIONS PAGE 176-7

PUZZLE 5

Which Morse code letter is missing from this sequence?

HOW RUDE!

'Flipping the bird' when someone takes your photo could be seen as a bit of fun. But in 1968, it became another example of steganography. The USS *Pueblo*, an American naval intelligence ship, had been captured by the North Korean military, who then staged a propaganda photo of some of the ship's crew. Under threat of harsh reprisals, the Americans were not able to convey their true situation. However, to show that they were only complying under duress, some of the crew secretly 'gave the finger' to the camera – a gesture that appeared to mean nothing to the North Koreans!

PUZZLE 6

Place a mine into some of the empty cells so that each number represents the total count of mines in neighbouring cells, including diagonally adjacent cells.

	2			1		1
	3	4	4		3	
2					4	
3		4	3		3	
				2		2
2		2			3	
	2					

PUZZLE 7

The year is 1975. Two friends, Bob and Frank, visit a bar in Milwaukee for the first time.

'*I'll have a beer please,*' says Bob.

'*Special or Lite?*' asks the bartender.

'*What's the difference?*' asks Bob.

'*Beats me,*' replies the bartender. '*Special is a dollar, Lite is ninety cents.*'

'*I'll take a Special,*' says Bob, handing over a dollar.

Frank watches his friend sip the foamy brew, then turns to the bar.

'*What'll it be?*' asks the bartender.

'*A beer please,*' says Frank, handing the bartender a dollar.

Without seeking clarification, the bartender pours him a Special.

Why didn't the bartender enquire after Frank's preference?

SOLUTIONS PAGE 177-8

PUZZLE 8

The best weapons against steganography are knowledge and observation. Crosswords and word search puzzles are a great way to test these abilities. Hidden in the word search below are 15 words relating to codes and ciphers. The words may appear horizontally, vertically or diagonally, backwards or forwards. Can you find them all?

I	G	B	H	F	J	F	K	E	N	R	R	H	G	G
T	Q	T	Y	O	A	I	N	N	N	A	F	Y	S	O
R	J	K	M	K	D	C	K	F	O	B	K	H	S	Q
E	W	C	O	J	R	A	Z	N	I	Y	S	P	I	X
B	M	G	K	Y	F	T	B	O	T	A	F	A	S	J
L	E	T	P	K	S	B	P	I	I	L	C	R	Y	B
A	S	T	R	V	E	A	E	T	S	P	E	G	L	P
V	S	B	F	D	T	S	K	U	O	H	G	O	A	X
V	A	W	M	L	R	H	A	T	P	A	R	N	N	X
T	G	H	E	O	L	C	Y	I	S	B	U	A	A	S
P	E	D	M	C	E	U	C	T	N	E	D	G	P	H
E	O	M	D	C	K	B	N	S	A	T	V	E	K	I
C	C	K	S	M	K	U	Q	B	R	W	Q	T	W	F
P	D	S	R	B	K	E	V	U	T	N	O	S	S	T
Z	H	E	N	A	W	J	Y	S	M	R	D	W	C	O

You can either work out the words from your general knowledge and sifting through the word search or come back to this and decipher the list below using the Atbash cipher you will come across later (see page 21).

ZOYVIGR
ZOKSZYVG
ZMZOBHRH
ZGYZHS
XRKSVI
XLWV
VMXIBKG
PVB
NVHHZTV
NLIHV
MFOO
HSRUG
HGVTZMLTIZKSB
HFYHGRGFGRLM
GIZMHKLHRGRLM

SCRAMBLE YOUR MESSAGE WITH CRYPTOGRAPHY

Steganography's effectiveness depends entirely upon drawing attention away from the message itself. But what happens if, despite all efforts, the message falls into enemy hands?

Ideally, your communication should be unintelligible to anyone but the intended recipient. Might it be possible to create a secret language that only you and your trusted allies understand?

Conversely, if your enemy has created such a language, how can you read their intercepted communications?

These questions are at the heart of cryptography – the art and science of secret writing.

CODE NAMES

A code name is a straight substitution of a word or phrase for something that has no connection to the subject. For example, Operation 'Market Garden' might sound like something horticultural but was in fact a military operation during the Second World War: 'Market' referred to an airborne assault intended to seize key bridges in the Netherlands, while 'Garden' was the advance of ground troops to consolidate this objective. The cunning code name, however, did not ensure the success of Operation 'Market Garden', which, sadly, failed. Of course, if subterfuge is not a priority, you can be less subtle; no one was under any misapprehension that Operation 'Desert Storm' referred to a study of weather conditions and landscapes.

SOLUTIONS PAGE 178

CIPHERS DECIPHERED

Cryptographers enjoy transforming simplicity into complexity and vice versa, so it is unsurprising that their field is replete with jargon:

A cipher is an ***algorithm*** *used to* ***encrypt*** *your* ***plaintext****. The person receiving your* ***ciphertext*** *can only* ***decrypt*** *it by using the same* ***algorithm*** *and the same* ***key****.*

In plain English:
A cipher is a ***system*** *used to* ***scramble*** *your* ***original message****. The person receiving your* ***scrambled*** *message can only* ***unscramble*** *it by using the same* ***system*** *and the same* ***method****.*

THE KEY IS THE KEY

If your cipher is good, it will become widely used. This, of course, means your enemies will eventually get to know of it too. According to American mathematician Claude Shannon, 'One ought to design systems under the assumption that the enemy will immediately gain full familiarity with them.'

So, your cipher needs a customisable element known only to the person who encrypts the message and the people who are *supposed* to decipher it. This element is called the 'key'. The more keys a cipher has, the greater its security.

CRACK IT: CRYPTANALYSIS

Sending and receiving secret messages is only half of the story. Just as a sound military strategy requires an understanding of both attack and defence, so anyone with a serious interest in secret messages must consider how they can be broken. Many of the puzzles in this book encourage you to look for weaknesses in encoded information and attack them mercilessly!

PUZZLE 9

You receive a mysterious transmission that appears to be extra-terrestrial in origin. What is missing from the sequence below?

Dah-Dah

Di-di-di-dah

Dah-Dah

Di-dah-dah-dah

Di-di-dit

Di-di-dah

Dah-dit

PUZZLE 10

Can you insert the letters C, O, D, E and S into the grid below so that the same letter does not occur more than once on the same column, row or long diagonal?

D				O
		D		
	O		E	
		S		
E				S

MOVE THE LETTERS: TRANSPOSITION

In a transposition cipher you encrypt your original message, or plaintext, by changing the positions of the letters. It is believed this system was first used to encrypt messages around 400 BCE by the Greeks, who were also fans of another entertaining form of transposition – the anagram.

SOLUTIONS PAGE 179

The Spartans used a cylindrical baton called a *scytale* to send secret military messages. A ribbon of parchment was wrapped around the scytale and the message written onto it. When the ribbon was unwound, the letters became jumbled. Only by winding the parchment around a scytale of the same diameter (which acted as the key) could the message be quickly decrypted.

PUZZLE 11

Each letter of the alphabet has been encrypted to a number (1 to 26). Crack the code to solve the puzzle and reveal the long thematic word hidden somewhere within the grid. To start you off, the codes for three letters have been given.

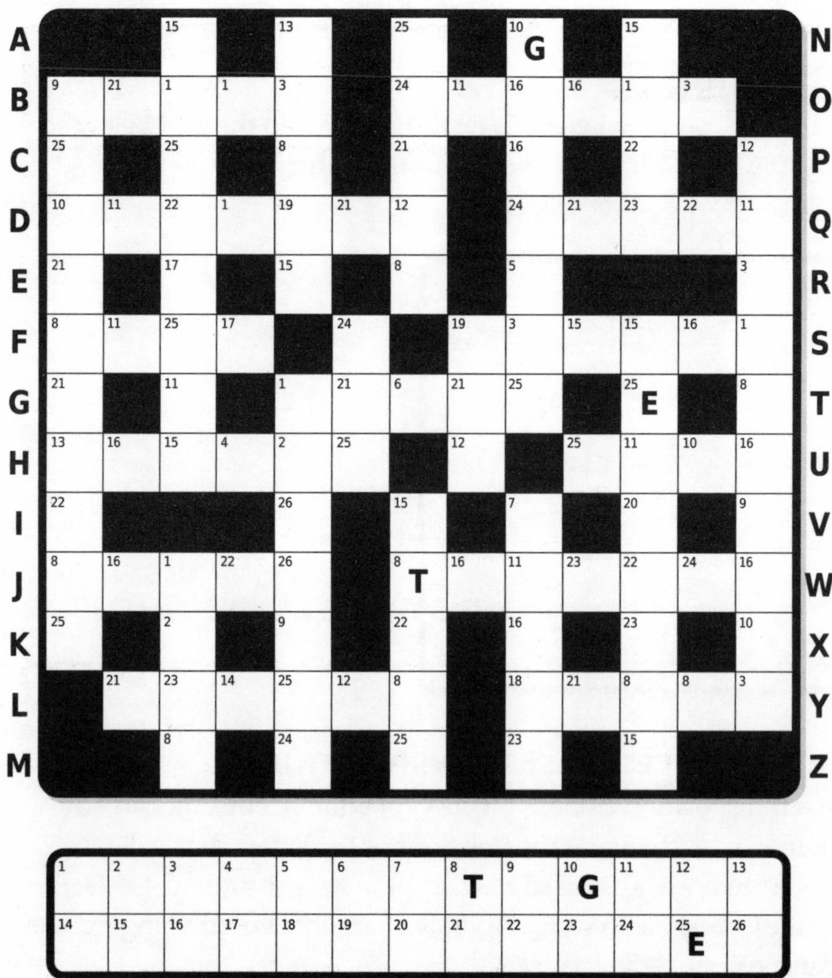

RAIL FENCE CIPHER

In this simple transposition cipher your plaintext is entered letter by letter onto the rows, or rails, of a grid, from left to right in a zig-zag pattern. The number of rails used is the key.

For example: you encrypt a message using a three-rail fence cipher and send the following ciphertext to your ally. The letters are grouped into blocks of five to make them easier to read.

TIETS HSSSC EMSAE IAREG

Your ally puts the letters onto the rail fence and reads from top left in a zig-zag pattern.

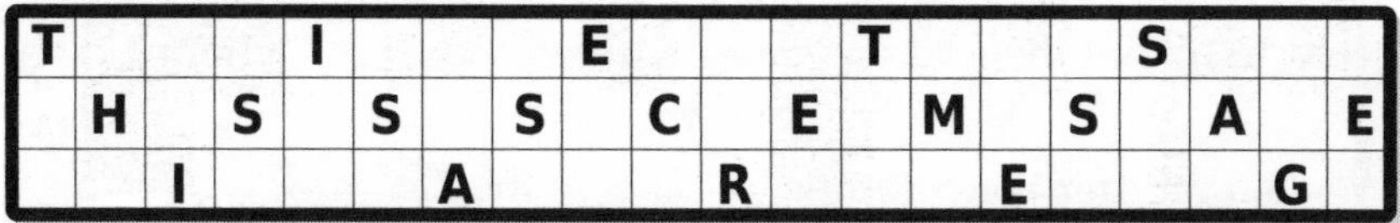

The spaces have been removed, but it takes little effort to get the original plaintext:

THIS IS A SECRET MESSAGE

PUZZLE 12

You receive a speedy and appropriate response from your ally. Can you decrypt it using the rail fence cipher?

WTKRH ELHNS ONTIG LAFON

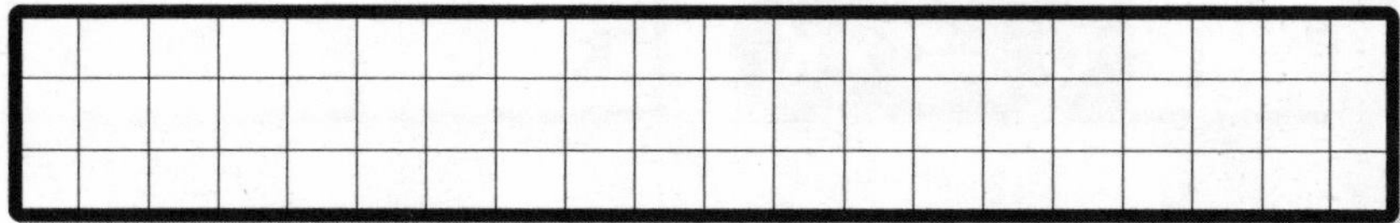

SOLUTIONS PAGE 179-80

COLUMNAR TRANSPOSITION

In this transposition cipher, the letters of the message are entered into a grid. The key is a word which tells you both how many columns are in the grid and their order. For example:

Our plaintext is:

THIS MESSAGE IS TOP SECRET

Our key is:

COBRA

Note: to fill out the grid we have included some junk letters (QXK).

We then reorder the columns by putting the key into alphabetical order.

C	O	B	R	A
T	H	I	S	M
E	S	S	A	G
E	I	S	T	O
P	S	E	C	R
E	T	Q	X	K

A	B	C	O	R
M	I	T	H	S
G	S	E	S	A
O	S	E	I	T
R	E	P	S	C
K	Q	E	T	X

Finally, we generate the ciphertext by reading off the columns from top to bottom and left to right:

M G O R K I S S E Q T E E P E H S I S T S A T C X

PUZZLE 13

You have received intelligence that your enemy likes to use keys with a hellish theme. Previous keywords have been: **HADES**, **FIEND** and **BEAST**.

Can you make a guess at the latest key and decrypt this ciphertext?

CUUKRHAPPIOOYCHSSLOKEFCXNITDMO

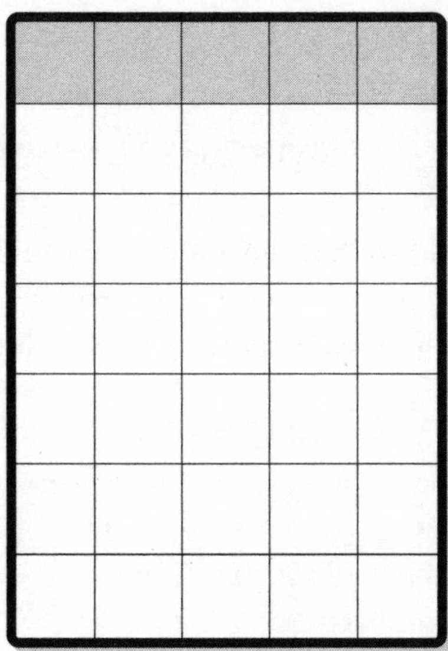

CHANGE THE LETTERS: SUBSTITUTION

In a substitution cipher, the letters of the plaintext remain in the same position but are substituted for different letters or symbols. The key tells the sender and receiver which letter relates to what.

The simplest type of substitution cipher is monoalphabetic, whereby each letter is substituted for another according to a fixed system.

ATBASH אתבש

This simple monoalphabetic cipher was developed by Hebrew scholars around 600 BCE and could be the oldest in existence. In Atbash, each letter of the plaintext alphabet is substituted for one from the ciphertext alphabet, which runs in reverse. The cipher's name is derived from the first and second letters (A → T, B → SH).

SOLUTIONS PAGE 180

Plaintext																					
ALEPH	BET	GIMEL	DALETH	HEH	VAV	ZAYIN	HET	TET	YODH	KAPH	LAMED	MEM	NUN	SAMECH	AYIN	PEH	TZADY	KOOF	REISH	SHIN	TAW
א	ב	ג	ד	ה	ו	ז	ח	ט	י	כ	ל	מ	נ	ס	ע	פ	צ	ק	ר	ש	ת
ת	ש	ר	ק	צ	פ	ע	ס	נ	מ	ל	כ	י	ט	ח	ז	ו	ה	ד	ג	ב	א
TAW	SHIN	REISH	KOOF	TZADY	PEH	AYIN	SAMECH	NUN	MEM	LAMED	KAPH	YODH	TET	HET	ZAYIN	VAV	HEH	DALETH	GIMEL	BET	ALEPH
Ciphertext																					

You can find examples of Atbash in the Old Testament:

'All the kings of the North, far and near, one with another; and all the kingdoms of the world which are on the face of the earth. Also, the king of ***Sheshach*** *shall drink after them.'* *Jeremiah 25:26 (NKJV)*

There is no record of a place called 'Sheshach' but there is of its decrypted form: Babylon.

Although Atbash was created for the Hebrew alphabet, it can be easily applied to the English one:

Plaintext												
a	**b**	**c**	**d**	**e**	**f**	**g**	**h**	**i**	**j**	**k**	**l**	**m**
Z	Y	X	W	V	U	T	S	R	Q	P	O	N
Ciphertext												
Plaintext												
n	**o**	**p**	**q**	**r**	**s**	**t**	**u**	**v**	**w**	**x**	**y**	**z**
M	L	K	J	I	H	G	F	E	D	C	B	A
Ciphertext												

Plaintext: **this message is not very secure**

Ciphertext: **GSRH NVHHZTV RH MLG EVIB HVXFIV**

Atbash does not use a key, which makes it easy to break – all you need to know is the system, or algorithm.

PUZZLE 14

Can you convert the four Hebrew letters inscribed on this tablet into single digit numbers so that the sum adds up?

PUZZLE 15

To make a cipher like Atbash more secure, it is a good idea to use it in conjunction with another algorithm. The message below is double encrypted using Atbash and a three-rail fence cipher (key = 3). Can you decipher it?

GVPZIUZVSVXMVKHXVRGLIWZIZVVGDVW

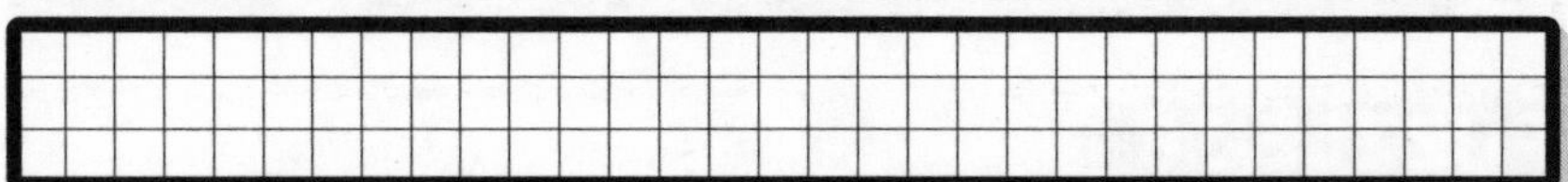

SOLUTIONS PAGE 180

THE CAESAR SHIFT CIPHER

One of the best-known substitution ciphers is the one purportedly used by, and named after, Julius Caesar. In the Caesar shift cipher each letter is substituted for another letter a fixed number of positions along in the alphabet.

The key is the number of shifts. Caesar is said to have preferred a shift of three letters to the right for his encoded communications:

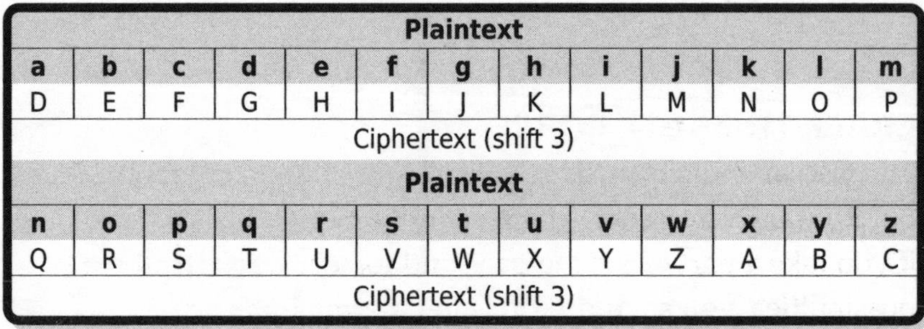

Plaintext												
a	**b**	**c**	**d**	**e**	**f**	**g**	**h**	**i**	**j**	**k**	**l**	**m**
D	E	F	G	H	I	J	K	L	M	N	O	P
Ciphertext (shift 3)												
Plaintext												
n	**o**	**p**	**q**	**r**	**s**	**t**	**u**	**v**	**w**	**x**	**y**	**z**
Q	R	S	T	U	V	W	X	Y	Z	A	B	C
Ciphertext (shift 3)												

So, if we take our plaintext message:

yet another secret message

and encrypt it using the three-letter shift key, we get the following ciphertext:

BHW DQRWKHU VHFUHW PHVVDJH

TIP

When encrypting and decrypting, it can be useful to put your plaintext and ciphertext in different cases to tell them apart.

PUZZLE 16

A substitution cipher was used to encrypt this message. Can you decrypt it?

N HFRJ N XFB N HTSVZJWJI

Clue: V for victory.  ____________________

PUZZLE 17

Determine what each of these sentences refers to. Then, put them in order to find the answer.

1. A spirit named after water. ....
2. A smart speaker from Amazon. ....
3. A course for potential Christians. ....
4. A club for American environmentalists. ....
5. A month for scorpions and archers. ....
6. A star-crossed lover. ....

CRACK IT: BRUTE FORCE

The Caesar shift cipher is a great introduction to cryptography but it is far from secure. There are only 25 possible shifts, so if you take a part of the message and force it through all the possibilities, you should be able to determine the key.

Let us attack some ciphertext using this method:

ZYPXFDEDETWWSLGPNSLZDTYZYPDPWQE
ZMPLMWPEZRTGPMTCESEZLOLYNTYRDELC

Shift	Plaintext	Shift	Plaintext
0	zypxfde	13	mlcksqr
1	yxowecd	14	lkbjrpq
2	xwnvdbc	15	kjaiqop
3	wvmucab	16	jizhpno
4	vultbza	17	ihygomn
5	utksayz	18	hgxfnlm
7	tsjrzxy	19	gfwemkl
6	sriqywx	20	fevdljk
8	rqhpxvw	21	educkij
9	qpgowuv	22	dctbjhi
10	pofnvtu	23	cbsaigh
11	**onemust**	24	barzhfg
12	nmdltrs	25	azqygef

The 11-shift plaintext looks suspiciously like English. If you apply that key to the entire message and add spaces, you get the following quote from Friedrich Nietzsche:

'One must still have chaos in oneself to be able to give birth to a dancing star.'

SOLUTIONS PAGE 181

PUZZLE 18

Apply some brute force to decipher this famous quote:

Y H Q L Y L G L Y L F L

Clue: You have seen this before, only in English.

PUZZLE 19

Which number is missing from the sequence?

3	3	5	4	4	____	5	5	4	3	6	6

PUZZLE 20

Shade the cells so that each number represents the total number of shaded cells touching that cell, including diagonally, and including itself. Is anything revealed?

2	4		4			2	3	2		
	5				6	3		4	7	4
2	3	2		3			4			
	5		4	4						4
		2		3	5		2	2		
	4	3		2		2	4	3	4	2
	5	4			7				7	4
2	3	2	4	4			5			3
4	5				7	4				
3				2				2	4	3

THE MASONIC CIPHER

A substitution cipher does not have to substitute letters for other letters – you can also use symbols. Morse code and Braille are substitution alphabets but their value as ciphers is limited because they are widely known.

The Masonic cipher (also known as the pigpen cipher) has the same weaknesses as other monoalphabetic systems, but, due to its elegance, it deserves a mention. The symbols are derived from fragments of grids that are superimposed over the letters.

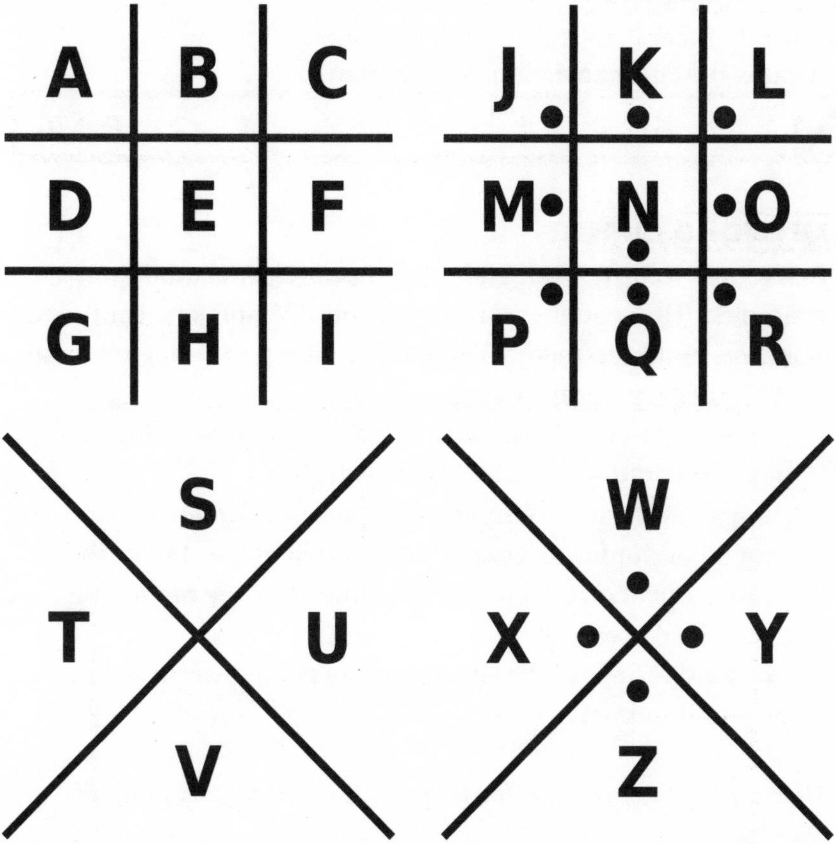

A	B	C
D	E	F
G	H	I

J•	K•	L•
M•	N•	•O
•P	•Q	•R

S
T U
V

W•
X• •Y
•Z

It might not be very secret, but it is rather pretty.

SOLUTIONS PAGE 181-2

PUZZLE 21

Three salesmen meet at a conference. Their name badges identify them as Mr Lee, Mr James and Mr Winston.

After a drink at the bar, formalities are dropped, and Mr Lee observes:

'What an incredible coincidence! Our first names are Lee, James and Winston.'

'That's true,' says James. *'Fortunately, none of us has the same first name as their last name!'*

What is the full name of each salesman?

KEYWORD CIPHER

To increase security, your ciphertext needs to be thoroughly scrambled. The sender and recipient could simply create random alphabets and keep them written down. But possessing physical evidence of cryptography might be dangerous. Memorizing a ciphertext alphabet is possible, but if you need to change it regularly, it could become a literal headache.

Using a keyword is a cunning compromise. A regular word is stripped of duplicate letters then inserted at the start of the ciphertext alphabet, which is then followed by the remaining letters in the correct order.

For example, let us take another quote from the nineteenth-century philosopher:

'Blessed are the forgetful for they get the better even of their blunders.'

The key is **NIETZSCHE** (removing the duplicate 'E')

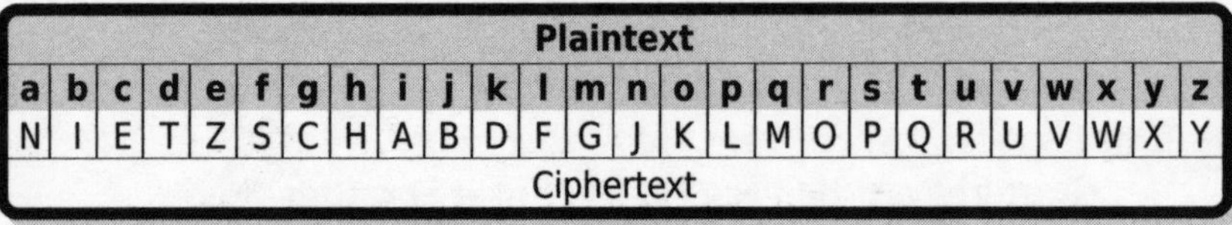

Plaintext																									
a	b	c	d	e	f	g	h	i	j	k	l	m	n	o	p	q	r	s	t	u	v	w	x	y	z
N	I	E	T	Z	S	C	H	A	B	D	F	G	J	K	L	M	O	P	Q	R	U	V	W	X	Y
Ciphertext																									

This gives us the following ciphertext:

IFZPPZT NOZ QHZ SKOCZQSRF SKO QHZX CZQ QHZ IZQQZO ZUZJ KS QHZAO IFRJTZOP

There are millions of alphabets that can be thus derived. It would take an eternity to decrypt a keyword ciphertext using brute force alone.

PUZZLE 22

Here is another famous quote encrypted using the keyword cipher. To find the keyword, you must decipher a clue that has been encrypted in Atbash.

AH TCH NCGMBH TCGT YOU WESC TO SHH EM TCH WORKD

Clue: NZSZGNZ YZKF  ____________________

CRACK IT: FREQUENCY ANALYSIS

A multi-talented ninth-century Islamic philosopher by the name of Al-Kindi noted a major weakness in all monoalphabetic substitution ciphers. Because each plaintext letter is always replaced by the same ciphertext letter, the ciphertext letter will appear as many times in the message as its equivalent. If certain letters occur more often in a language than others, we can make an educated guess regarding their substitution.

Here is a frequency analysis of the alphabet letters in English, given as a percentage of occurrences:

12.7	9.1	8.2	7.5	7.0	6.7	6.3	6.1	6.0	4.3	4.0	2.8	2.8
E	T	A	O	I	N	S	H	R	D	L	C	U
2.4	2.4	2.2	2.0	2.0	1.9	1.5	1.0	0.8	0.2	0.2	0.1	0.1
M	W	F	G	Y	P	B	V	K	J	X	Q	Z

There are also commonly occurring groups of letters:

Digraphs: TH, HE, AN, IN, ER, ON, RE, ED, ND, HA, AT, EN, EA
Doubles: SS, EE, TT, FF, LL, MM, OO
Trigraphs: THE, AND, THA, ENT, ION, TIO, FOR, NDE, HAS, NCE, TIS, OFT, MEN

SOLUTIONS PAGE 182

Let us see if we can use this to crack some ciphertext. We shall keep ciphertext letters in CAPS and plaintext in lower case.

AI LSPH XLIWI XVYXLW XS FI WIPJ-IZMHIRX, XLEX EPP QIR EVI GVIEXIH IUYEP, XLEX XLIC EVI IRHSAIH FC XLIMV GVIEXSV AMXL GIVXEMR YREPMIREFPI VMKLXW, XLEX EQSRK XLIWI EVI PMJI, PMFIVXC ERH XLI TYVWYMX SJ LETTMRIWW. XLEX XS WIGYVI XLIWI VMKLXW, KSZIVRQIRXW EVI MRWXMXYXIH EQSRK QIR, HIVMZMRK XLIMV NYWX TSAIVW JVSQ XLI GSRWIRX SJ XLI KSZIVRIH,--XLEX ALIRIZIV ERC JSVQ SJ KSZIVRQIRX FIGSQIW HIWXVYGXMZI SJ XLIWI IRHW, MX MW XLI VMKLX SJ XLI TISTPI XS EPXIV SV XS EFSPMWL MX, ERH XS MRWXMXYXI RIA KSZIVRQIRX, PECMRK MXW JSYRHEXMSR SR WYGL TVMRGMTPIW ERH SVKERMDMRK MXW TSAIVW MR WYGL JSVQ, EW XS XLIQ WLEPP WIIQ QSWX PMOIPC XS IJJIGX XLIMV WEJIXC ERH LETTMRIWW.

First look at the two most common letters in English – E and T – and the two most common letters in the message below: *I* (77 instances) and *X* (65 instances). What happens if we make a straight substitution?

Ae LSPH tLeWe tVYtLW tS Fe WePJ-eZMHeRt, tLEt EPP QeR EVe GVeEteH eUYEP, tLEt tLeC EVe eRHSAeH FC tLeMV GVeEtSV AMtL GeVtEMR YREPMeREFPe VMKLtW, tLEt EQSRK tLeWe EVe PMJe, PMFeVtC ERH tLe TYVWYMt SJ LETTMReWW. tLEt tS WeGYVe tLeWe VMKLtW, KSZeVRQeRtW EVe MRWtMtYteH EQSRK QeR, HeVMZMRK tLeMV NYWt TSAeVW JVSQ tLe GSRWeRt SJ tLe KSZeVReH,--tLEt ALeReZeV ERC JSVQ SJ KSZeVRQeRt FeGSQeW HeWtVYGtMZe SJ tLeWe eRHW, Mt MW tLe VMKLt SJ tLe TeSTPe tS EPteV SV tS EFSPMWL Mt, ERH tS MRWtMtYte ReA KSZeVRQeRt, PECMRK MtW JSYRHEtMSR SR WYGL TVMRGMTPeW ERH SVKERMDMRK MtW TSAeVW MR WYGL JSVQ, EW tS tLeQ WLEPP WeeQ QSWt PMOePC tS eJJeGt tLeMV WEJetC ERH LETTMReWW.

For the moment, assume that these frequencies tally (they do, in fact) and see if you can find a commonly occurring trigraph in English ('the') and a commonly occurring adjective ('that').

Good candidates would seem to be *tLe* and *tLEt* respectively. So, we substitute 'h' for *L* and 'a' for *E*:

Ae hSPH theWe tVYthW tS Fe WePJ-eZMHeRt, that aPP QeR aVe GVeateH eUYaP, that theC aVe eRHSAeH FC theMV GVeatSV AMth GeVtaMR YRaPMeRaFPe VMKhtW, that aQSRK theWe aVe PMJe, PMFeVtC aRH the TYVWYMt SJ haTTMReWW. that tS WeGYVe theWe VMKhtW, KSZeVRQeRtW aVe MRWtMtYteH aQSRK QeR, HeVMZMRK theMV NYWt TSAeVW JVSQ the GSRWeRt SJ the KSZeVReH,--that AheReZeV aRC JSVQ SJ KSZeVRQeRt FeGSQeW HeWtVYGtMZe SJ theWe eRHW, Mt MW the VMKht SJ the TeSTPe tS aPteV SV tS aFSPMWh Mt, aRH tS MRWtMtYte ReA KSZeVRQeRt, PaCMRK MtW JSYRHatMSR SR WYGh TVMRGMTPeW aRH SVKaRMDMRK MtW TSAeVW MR WYGh JSVQ, aW tS theQ WhaPP WeeQ QSWt PMOePC tS eJJeGt theMV WaJetC aRH haTTMReWW.

This is starting to look promising! We can deduce that *tS* must be 'to' and *aPP* can either be 'ass' or 'all' – so let's plug in the latter:

Ae holH theWe tVYthW to Fe WelJ-eZMHeRt, that all QeR aVe GVeateH eUYal, that theC aVe eRHoAeH FC theMV GVeatoV AMth GeVtaMR YRalMeRaFle VMKhtW, that aQoRK theWe aVe lMJe, lMFeVtC aRH the TYVWYMt oJ haTTMReWW. that to WeGYVe theWe VMKhtW, KoZeVRQeRtW aVe MRWtMtYteH aQoRK QeR, HeVMZMRK theMV NYWt ToAeVW JVoQ the GoRWeRt oJ the KoZeVReH,--that AheReZeV aRC JoVQ oJ KoZeVRQeRt FeGoQeW HeWtVYGtMZe oJ theWe eRHW, Mt MW the VMKht oJ the TeoTle to alteV oV to aFolMWh Mt, aRH to MRWtMtYte ReA KoZeVRQeRt, laCMRK MtW JoYRHatMoR oR WYGh TVMRGMTleW aRH oVKaRMDMRK MtW ToAeVW MR WYGh JoVQ, aW to theQ Whall WeeQ QoWt lMOelC to eJJeGt theMV WaJetC aRH haTTMReWW.

PUZZLE 23

Continue looking for patterns and frequencies and see if you can decrypt the rest of the text. If you get stuck, try one of the transposition ciphers that we looked at in the previous section.

SOLUTIONS PAGE 183

PUZZLE 24

You are given the task of bringing back *exactly* four pints of water from a spring. But you only have two unmarked containers: a jug that can hold up to five pints; and a jar that can hold up to three pints.

How can you bring back exactly four pints, no more, no less?

THE ALBERTI CIPHER

In 1467, an Italian architect by the name of Leon Battista Alberti made a significant improvement to the substitution method and invented one of the first polyalphabetic ciphers – an effective defence against frequency analysis.

Rather than rely on pages of different alphabets, he created an ingenious code wheel. The plaintext alphabet is on the static outer wheel, while the ciphertext alphabet is on a moveable inner wheel.

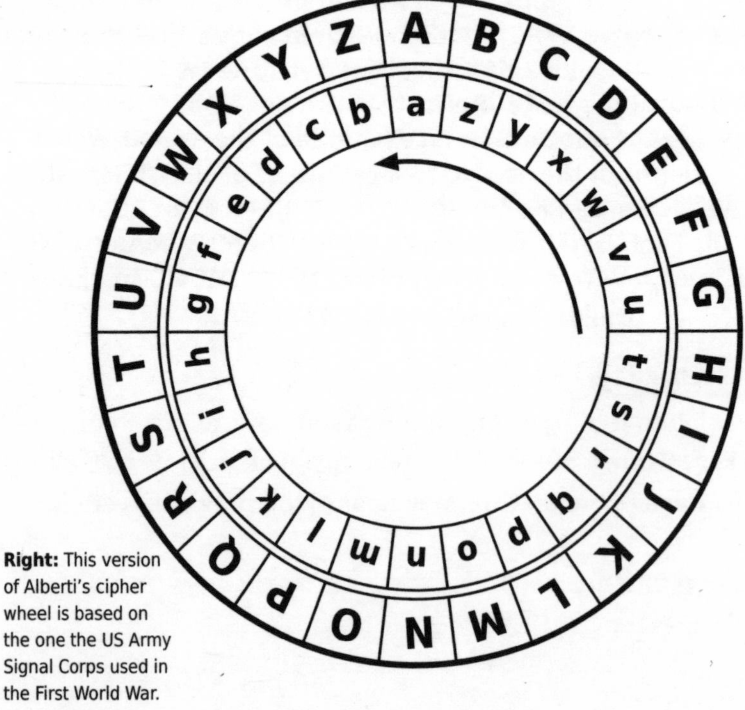

Right: This version of Alberti's cipher wheel is based on the one the US Army Signal Corps used in the First World War.

MAKE YOUR OWN CIPHER DISK
Photocopy or cut out the two wheels in the picture section of the book. Line up the smaller wheel in the centre of the larger one and put a drawing pin through the dot in the centre.

Having a letter substitute for itself is not ideal. Align the outer 'A' with the inner 'a', as shown in the illustration, then rotate the inner wheel anti-clockwise so that 'A' aligns with 'z', for a shift of one. This, coincidentally, gives us the same ciphertext alphabet as Atbash.

Plaintext												
a	b	c	d	e	f	g	h	i	j	k	l	m
Z	Y	X	W	V	U	T	S	R	Q	P	O	N
Ciphertext (Shift 1)												
Plaintext												
n	o	p	q	r	s	t	u	v	w	x	y	z
M	L	K	J	I	H	G	F	E	D	C	B	A
Ciphertext (Shift 1)												

From here on, the clues to certain puzzles will be encrypted with Atbash – set your cipher wheel to shift 1 to read them.

PUZZLE 25

Your enemy is a notorious lover of anagrams. We have intercepted the following message, which was encrypted with the Vigenère cipher (see page 35), along with the keyword SILENT. However, the decrypted message makes no sense!

OWFHXGPTDLIPCMLLXBEPGLIJSWKXJNTBZTR QDQDXRPPGGNLNGMFHXNWZWTHLEMKMIQ

Can you get into the mind of your enemy and decrypt the message?

SOLUTIONS PAGE 183

The strength of Alberti's cipher wheel is that it allows you to change the ciphertext alphabet within a single message – this is what makes it polyalphabetic. There are various ways to encrypt a message using the wheel. Here is just one example:

Both sender and receiver must agree on three numbers:

- The **start**. The initial number of shifts. If 'A' → 'a' is start zero, then 'A' → 'z' is start 1.
- The **length**. How many letters of plaintext will be encrypted before the wheel is rotated?
- The **increment**. How many letter shifts will be made on each rotation?

For example, you want to encrypt the following plaintext message:

THISMESSAGEISHARDERTODECIPHER

You decide to use a length 5 which breaks the message up into six chunks:

THISM ESSAG EISHA RDERT ODECI PHER

You have also decided on start 1 and increment 2, so the six chunks will be encrypted like this:

Your final ciphertext looks like this:

GSRHN TFFXR RNDOV CQPCA DONPJ AILY

Plaintext																									
a	**b**	**c**	**d**	**e**	**f**	**g**	**h**	**i**	**j**	**k**	**l**	**m**	**n**	**o**	**p**	**q**	**r**	**s**	**t**	**u**	**v**	**w**	**x**	**y**	**z**
Z	Y	X	W	V	U	T	S	R	Q	P	O	N	M	L	K	J	I	H	G	F	E	D	C	B	A
X	W	V	U	T	S	R	Q	P	O	N	M	L	K	J	I	H	G	F	E	D	C	B	A	Z	Y
V	U	T	S	R	Q	P	O	N	M	L	K	J	I	H	G	F	E	D	C	B	A	Z	Y	X	W
T	S	R	Q	P	O	N	M	L	K	J	I	H	G	F	E	D	C	B	A	Z	Y	X	W	V	U
R	Q	P	O	N	M	L	K	J	I	H	G	F	E	D	C	B	A	Z	Y	X	W	V	U	T	S
P	O	N	M	L	K	J	I	H	G	F	E	D	C	B	A	Z	Y	X	W	V	U	T	S	R	Q
Ciphertext																									

PUZZLE 26

Time to try out your wheel! Your ally has sent you the following important message.

QFONFIHDEZYVLCHVHTZJA

The key is: 1/2/3. Can you decipher it?

THE VIGENÈRE CIPHER

In 1553, another Italian cryptologist, Giovan Battista Bellaso, made a further advancement in polyalphabetic substitution – an algorithm so cunning it became known as 'the indecipherable cipher'. Today, it is referred to as the Vigenère cipher because its creation was wrongly credited to another cryptographer, Blaise de Vigenère.

The key is derived from the table overleaf, which corresponds to the 25 shifts of the Caesar cipher.

PUZZLE 27

Can you find the names of five codes, or types of cipher, hidden in the following lines? For example, the word 'code' is hidden in the phrase 'spies in Mexico denied the allegation'. One word is hidden in each line.

1. The diplomat bashfully admitted to copying confidential documents.
2. Start by checking whether it's an anagram, or see if there are any letters missing.
3. For the first mission, he was the perfect guinea pig; pensive, hard-working and suspicious of everyone.
4. We can't afford to be slapdash if there's an issue of national security at stake.
5. You'll need to use intelligence from the Bureau to key in the right codes.

SOLUTIONS PAGE 184

	A	B	C	D	E	F	G	H	I	J	K	L	M	N	O	P	Q	R	S	T	U	V	W	X	Y	Z
A	A	B	C	D	E	F	G	H	I	J	K	L	M	N	O	P	Q	R	S	T	U	V	W	X	Y	Z
B	B	C	D	E	F	G	H	I	J	K	L	M	N	O	P	Q	R	S	T	U	V	W	X	Y	Z	A
C	C	D	E	F	G	H	I	J	K	L	M	N	O	P	Q	R	S	T	U	V	W	X	Y	Z	A	B
D	D	E	F	G	H	I	J	K	L	M	N	O	P	Q	R	S	T	U	V	W	X	Y	Z	A	B	C
E	E	F	G	H	I	J	K	L	M	N	O	P	Q	R	S	T	U	V	W	X	Y	Z	A	B	C	D
F	F	G	H	I	J	K	L	M	N	O	P	Q	R	S	T	U	V	W	X	Y	Z	A	B	C	D	E
G	G	H	I	J	K	L	M	N	O	P	Q	R	S	T	U	V	W	X	Y	Z	A	B	C	D	E	F
H	H	I	J	K	L	M	N	O	P	Q	R	S	T	U	V	W	X	Y	Z	A	B	C	D	E	F	G
I	I	J	K	L	M	N	O	P	Q	R	S	T	U	V	W	X	Y	Z	A	B	C	D	E	F	G	H
J	J	K	L	M	N	O	P	Q	R	S	T	U	V	W	X	Y	Z	A	B	C	D	E	F	G	H	I
K	K	L	M	N	O	P	Q	R	S	T	U	V	W	X	Y	Z	A	B	C	D	E	F	G	H	I	J
L	L	M	N	O	P	Q	R	S	T	U	V	W	X	Y	Z	A	B	C	D	E	F	G	H	I	J	K
M	M	N	O	P	Q	R	S	T	U	V	W	X	Y	Z	A	B	C	D	E	F	G	H	I	J	K	L
N	N	O	P	Q	R	S	T	U	V	W	X	Y	Z	A	B	C	D	E	F	G	H	I	J	K	L	M
O	O	P	Q	R	S	T	U	V	W	X	Y	Z	A	B	C	D	E	F	G	H	I	J	K	L	M	N
P	P	Q	R	S	T	U	V	W	X	Y	Z	A	B	C	D	E	F	G	H	I	J	K	L	M	N	O
Q	Q	R	S	T	U	V	W	X	Y	Z	A	B	C	D	E	F	G	H	I	J	K	L	M	N	O	P
R	R	S	T	U	V	W	X	Y	Z	A	B	C	D	E	F	G	H	I	J	K	L	M	N	O	P	Q
S	S	T	U	V	W	X	Y	Z	A	B	C	D	E	F	G	H	I	J	K	L	M	N	O	P	Q	R
T	T	U	V	W	X	Y	Z	A	B	C	D	E	F	G	H	I	J	K	L	M	N	O	P	Q	R	S
U	U	V	W	X	Y	Z	A	B	C	D	E	F	G	H	I	J	K	L	M	N	O	P	Q	R	S	T
V	V	W	X	Y	Z	A	B	C	D	E	F	G	H	I	J	K	L	M	N	O	P	Q	R	S	T	U
W	W	X	Y	Z	A	B	C	D	E	F	G	H	I	J	K	L	M	N	O	P	Q	R	S	T	U	V
X	X	Y	Z	A	B	C	D	E	F	G	H	I	J	K	L	M	N	O	P	Q	R	S	T	U	V	W
Y	Y	Z	A	B	C	D	E	F	G	H	I	J	K	L	M	N	O	P	Q	R	S	T	U	V	W	X
Z	Z	A	B	C	D	E	F	G	H	I	J	K	L	M	N	O	P	Q	R	S	T	U	V	W	X	Y

To encrypt your message, you also need a pre-agreed keyword. The keyword is written repeatedly until you have as many letters as there are in your message.

So, if we take a 20-letter plaintext message:

THIS IS A SECRET MESSAGE

And use the keyword SECRET, it will be applied to the message like so:

SECR ET S ECRETS ECRETSE

Now we encrypt each letter of the plaintext in turn using the alphabet corresponding to the keyword letter in the same position. So, the first letter of the plaintext 'T' will be encrypted in alphabet 'S' which gives us the ciphertext output 'L'.

Our finished ciphertext looks like this:

LLKJ ML S WGTVXL QGJWTYI

PUZZLE 28

This Sudoku has been encrypted with the letters **ADEILNPTX**. Solve it to find the word revealed in the shaded boxes.

						T	E	
		D			N			P
	N			I	E			X
				X		A		
		P	D		A	X		
		N		E				
A			N	L			D	
N			T			L		
	I	X						

SOLUTIONS PAGE 184

PUZZLE 29

A cash-strapped nicotine addict collects used cigarettes. He can make a new cigarette from the residual tobacco of any three used cigarettes.

If he has collected nine used cigarettes, how many new cigarettes can he enjoy?

PUZZLE 30

Which box (A, B, C or D) completes the grid below?

A	B	C	D
•• ——	——— •••	•• —•—	••• •

—••• —•—•	•—• —	• ••••	—•— ———
•• ——	— •——	•• —•—	••• —
••—• ••		•—• •••	• ——•
•••— —••—	•— —•••	•••• •—••	——— •—•

CRACK IT: ADVANCED FREQUENCY ANALYSIS

For centuries, the Vigenère cipher was regarded as impenetrable. In 1854, however, British cryptographer Charles Babbage found a weakness using a form of frequency analysis, plus a lot of hard work, patience and determination.

Look at this string of ciphertext. Do you notice any interesting repetitions?

CVLJJMHAMHORCFBGQOUQCVLYRTLAXCU
RLCTRBHVGQSMNCVLENLJRYHAUACBTQAL

The triad 'CVL' occurs three times and is preserved when the text is split into groups of four letters. So, it is possible that 'CVL' decrypts to the same plaintext word and that the key length is four.

CVLJ JMHA MHOR CFBG QOUQ **CVL**Y RTLA XCUR
LCTR BHVG QSMN **CVL**E NLJR YHAU ACBT QAL

What if 'CVL' was the frequently occurring word in English 'the'? This would lead us to conclude that the first three letters of the keyword are J O H.

	A	B	C	D	E	F	G	H	I	J	K	L	M	N	O	P	Q	R	S	T	U
A	a	b	c	d	e	f	g	h	i	j	k	l	m	n	o	p	q	r	s	t	u
B	b	c	d	e	f	g	h	i	j	k	l	m	n	o	p	q	r	s	t	u	v
C	c	d	e	f	g	h	i	j	k	l	m	n	o	p	q	r	s	t	u	v	w
D	d	e	f	g	h	i	j	k	l	m	n	o	p	q	r	s	t	u	v	w	x
E	e	f	g	h	i	j	k	l	m	n	o	p	q	r	s	t	u	v	w	x	y
F	f	g	h	i	j	k	l	m	n	o	p	q	r	s	t	u	v	w	x	y	z
G	g	h	i	j	k	l	m	n	o	p	q	r	s	t	u	v	w	x	y	z	a
H	h	i	j	k	l	m	n	o	p	q	r	s	t	u	v	w	x	y	z	a	b
I	i	j	k	l	m	n	o	p	q	r	s	t	u	v	w	x	y	z	a	b	c
J	j	k	l	m	n	o	p	q	r	s	t	u	v	w	x	y	z	a	b	c	d
K	k	l	m	n	o	p	q	r	s	t	u	v	w	x	y	z	a	b	c	d	e
L	l	m	n	o	p	q	r	s	t	u	v	w	x	y	z	a	b	c	d	e	f
M	m	n	o	p	q	r	s	t	u	v	w	x	y	z	a	b	c	d	e	f	g
N	n	o	p	q	r	s	t	u	v	w	x	y	z	a	b	c	d	e	f	g	h
O	o	p	q	r	s	t	u	v	w	x	y	z	a	b	c	d	e	f	g	h	i
P	p	q	r	s	t	u	v	w	x	y	z	a	b	c	d	e	f	g	h	i	j

Which we can then apply to the ciphertext:

theJ ayaA dthR truG hanQ theY ifeA oonR comR stoG hefN theE excR pttU rouT hme

We might now have enough decrypted text to work out the entire message, or we could finish the key – which we guess is 'JOHN'.

Putting in the correct spaces, we get the following extract from the New Testament.

the way and the truth and the life no one comes to the father except through me

SOLUTIONS PAGE 185

PUZZLE 31

Complete the Sudoku puzzle by inserting the letters A, B, C, D, E, F, G, H and I into the grid so that each letter only appears once in each column, each row and each block of nine squares.

Circle the nine letters in the shaded boxes.

			C	G				
A		C				H		
					A	F		D
I	C	B						
	A					E		C
			B					
H			I				E	B
		E	D				H	
D			G					I

Then do the same with this Sudoku, inserting the numbers 0, 1, 2, 3, 4, 5, 6, 7 and 8. In each block, add up the numbers in the shaded squares and apply that number as a Caesar shift to the circled letter in the corresponding block. The bottom centre block has already been decoded for you.

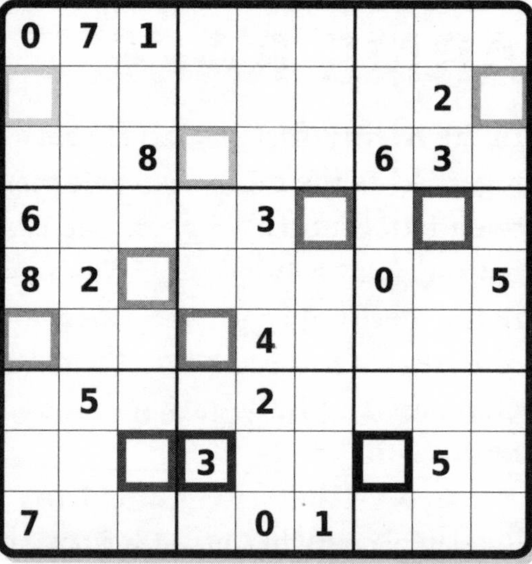

0	7	1						
							2	
		8				6	3	
6				3				
8	2					0		5
				4				
	5			2				
			3				5	
7				0	1			

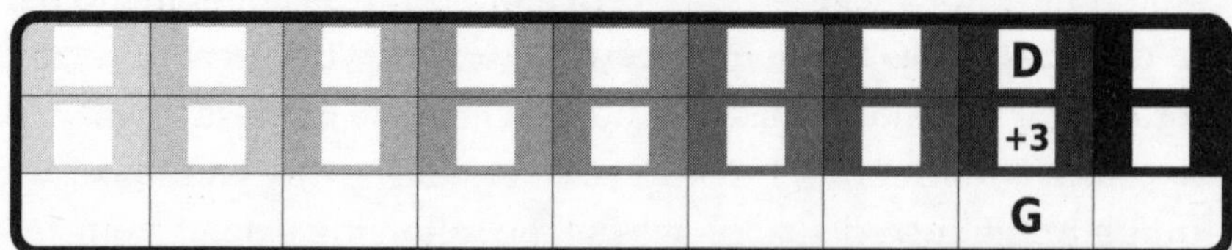

When you have all nine letters, unscramble them to create the mystery word.

SOLUTIONS PAGE 185

THE 'GREAT WAR'

The 'Great War' of 1914–1918 was a brutal conflict on a scale the world had never seen. Some 30 million military personnel were killed or wounded during the four years of fighting – not to mention the civilian toll – but there is still no consensus as to why it started. The best we can do is describe *how* it started.

ARMS RACE

In the twenty-first century, peace is almost universally regarded as the most desirable state. But at the start of the twentieth century, war was seen as a legitimate pursuit for nations who wanted to maintain or enhance their standing in the world. As a consequence, all the great powers of Europe – Britain, France, Russia, Austria-Hungary, Germany and Italy – at this time could be described as militaristic.

Russian playwright Anton Chekhov famously asserted that a gun should never be included early in a story if it was not going to be fired later. Thanks to the Industrial Revolution, the great powers of the early twentieth century had a *lot* of guns. With so much investment in firepower, it seemed likely that a way would be found to use these deadly new arsenals.

Germany and Britain had been engaged in a naval arms race since the end of the nineteenth century. Britain had the largest navy in the world at the time and adopted the 'two-power standard', meaning it strove to be as powerful as the next two largest navies combined. Two major reasons for this were Britain's need to safeguard its vast global Empire and that Britain itself was vulnerable as an island. Over half the food consumed in Britain came from overseas, and the maritime trade from its imperial colonies required constant protection.

When Germany increased its battleship production with the Naval Bill of 1908, Britain grew concerned and responded by increasing its own naval building programme. However, Germany's naval expenditure ran alongside investment in its army – one of the largest and best-resourced in Europe – which needed to be maintained because of the threat posed by its neighbour, Russia.

Russia had a standing army of one and a half million soldiers. When tensions began to boil over in 1914, it started to mobilise even before war was formally declared. Although not as industrialised as its rivals, Russia was absolutely determined to prove itself as a great power.

Military spending on battlefield technology resulted in weaponry becoming more accurate and lethal compared to the previous century. In the Napoleonic Wars (1803–1815), British infantrymen were issued with a Model 1793 India Pattern Musket which had an effective range of 45–55 metres and a rate of fire of three rounds per minute. In the 'Great War', British infantrymen received a Short Magazine Lee Enfield (SMLE) Mk.III (introduced in 1907. The simplified Mk.III* was introduced in 1915), which was deadlier, more accurate, and effective up to 503 metres. Its clip could hold five bullets, which could be discharged at a rate of 15 rounds per minute by a trained soldier – this was referred to as the 'mad minute' – or 25–30 in the hands of a truly expert marksman. Once the war began in earnest, weapons became rapidly more sophisticated.

PUZZLE 32

Can you complete this First World War-themed crossword?

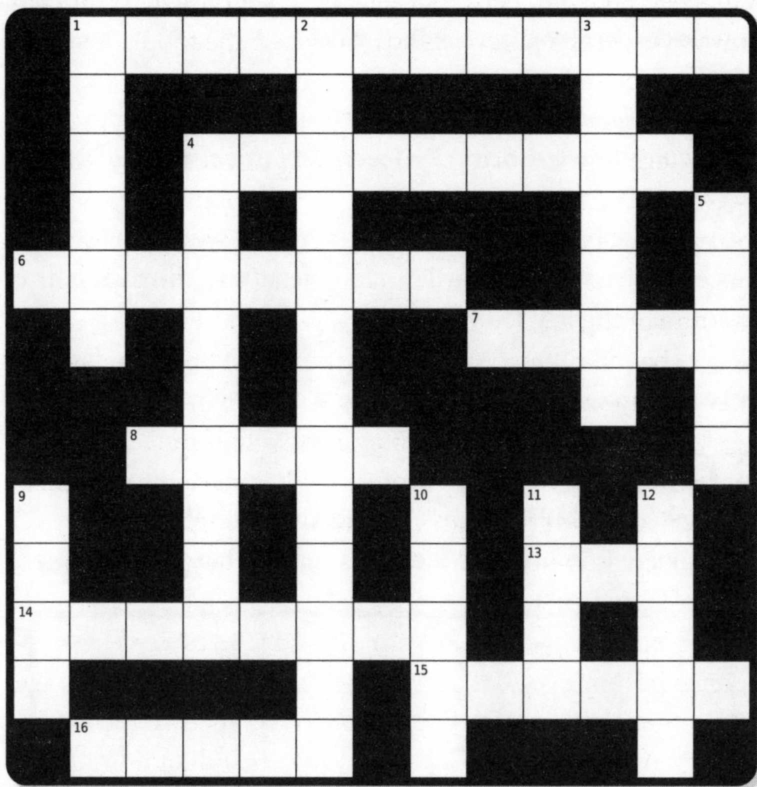

ACROSS

1 Type of gun used to attack enemy planes (4-8)
4 The national attempt to win (3,6)
6 Armed forces in general (8)
7 Observation balloon (5)
8 German submarine (1-4)
13 Highly regarded fighter pilot (3)
14 Burial site of a victim of armed conflict (3,5)
15 Gunfire from 1 across (3-3)
16 German soldier, informally, once upon a time (5)

DOWN

1 Informal name for 1 across (6)
2 Battles in the sky (6,7)
3 Attack on a location by enemy planes (3,4)
4 High velocity shell named after the sounds it made (5-4)
5 Used up or dead, in First World War military slang (5)
9 New Zealand soldier, informally (4)
10 Adjective for the First World War: The ___ War (5)
11 Armoured vehicle (4)
12 Preliminary inspection, in RAF slang (5)

SOLUTIONS PAGE 186

PUZZLE 33

Franz was a consummate sportsman who liked to make wagers based on his skill. One afternoon he had just returned from a hunt and was still carrying his fowling piece.

'I'll wager a gold mark that I can shoot a hole through my hat from where I am standing,' he announced. 'Furthermore, I will do it blindfolded!'

Glancing at the hat stand, which was some 70 metres in the distance at the end of the castle's main vestibule, the members of his entourage eagerly took up the bet.

Why was Franz so confident that he would win the wager?

PUZZLE 34

The letters **ACDENPRTY** have replaced the numbers in this Sudoku. Solve it to uncover the word revealed in the shaded boxes.

		R	Y			P		T
			E			R		
	P				R			
N				C	D			A
D			T	E				N
			D				P	
		Y			N			
R		T			Y	C		

PUZZLE 35

Battleships! Find the enemy fleet on the grid below. The numbers on the periphery tell you how many occupied squares are in that row or column. No two vessels occupy neighbouring squares (including diagonals). An X marks an empty square. There are four kinds of vessel, and the number of each type in the fleet is as follows:

Battleship ◀■■▶ x1
Cruiser ◀■▶ x2
Destroyer ◀▶ x3
Submarine ■ x4

	3	1	4	2	3	0	3	1	1	2	
4											4
2											2
0											0
1											1
2											2
4											4
4											4
0											0
3			X								3
0											0
	3	1	4	2	3	0	3	1	1	2	

SOLUTIONS PAGE 186-7

ALLIANCES

A disagreement between two nations might lead to a localised armed conflict, but when the belligerents have defensive pacts with other nations, a regional clash can escalate into something much larger. Before the outbreak of war, the six great powers of Europe were divided into two blocs: the Triple Alliance and the Triple Entente.

The Triple Alliance

Following on from victory in a war with France, the German states, led by the powerful kingdom of Prussia, unified into a single country and empire in 1871. Its chancellor, Otto von Bismarck, was determined to maintain German supremacy in Europe, which meant keeping a hostile France isolated and away from possible allies. Whilst working to maintain good relations between Germany and Russia, he brokered a defensive pact with Austria-Hungary and Italy in 1882, which became known as the Triple Alliance.

The Triple Entente

Having suffered defeat at the hands of newly powerful Germany, France needed allies. Serious disagreements over foreign policy with Germany's new emperor, Wilhelm II, led to Bismarck's forced resignation. Wilhelm's new direction, 'Weltpolitik' (World Policy) naval expansion, threatened Britain, as did Germany's alliance with Austria-Hungary threaten Russia. Both moved towards France and in 1907 the Triple Entente was established. The tables were turned, and it was now Germany which felt threatened by its powerful neighbours, even though the Triple Entente was not a formal defensive pact.

The Balkans

In south-eastern Europe, the Balkan peninsula comprised a cluster of economically underdeveloped nations, including Bulgaria, Greece, Montenegro and Serbia. With low populations and few industrial and military resources, the Balkans might have been overlooked by the great powers were it not for its strategic location: it shared borders with the Russian, Austria-Hungarian and the Ottoman Empires, and had access to the Mediterranean, the Adriatic, the Aegean and Black Seas.

Localised tension also resulted in conflicts in the region. Serbia was of particular importance to the Russian Empire as it constituted a geographical buffer against the regional expansion of its rival Austria-Hungary.

The Ottoman Empire

The Ottoman Empire had been a mighty caliphate for 600 years, but by the early twentieth century was in decline. With a largely agrarian economy, an under-educated population and a multi-cultural society that lacked patriotic cohesion, it knew its days were numbered. Picking the right side in the coming storm would be crucial. It had no true friends but plenty of rivals who wanted to hasten its demise.

The British were opposed to Russian expansion in the Balkans and so favoured keeping the Ottoman Empire as a buffer, but that did not stop them from undermining them whenever they could, for example by encouraging Arab nationalists who were already chafing against the Ottoman rule.

The United States

The United States had only recently emerged from its bloody Civil War (1861–65). By the turn of the century, however, it was enjoying an industrial and cultural boom. It was looking to expand its military and financial influence in the Caribbean and Pacific and wanted no part in the entangling alliances of Europe.

Japan

Great Britain signed an alliance with Japan in 1902, based on a mutual opposition to Russian expansion. The United States was unhappy with this since Japan was its main rival in the Pacific. The Anglo-Japanese alliance was far from stable but held together until 1923.

PUZZLE 36

In an alternative history, you have created an alliance between Germany, Austria-Hungary, Bulgaria, Romania, Italy and the Ottoman Empire. Your job, in the build-up to an inevitable war, is to keep your alliance happy or, at the very least, to prevent any of the members from becoming too angry. Condemning your mutual rivals is the key – but you must proceed with care.

If you condemn Russia, it will make Bulgaria and Germany happy, but will anger Austria-Hungary and Romania. If you condemn the United States, it will anger Italy, but Austria-Hungary and Romania will be happy. If you condemn Serbia, it will make Bulgaria and Austria-Hungary happy, but Romania, Germany and the Ottoman Empire will be angry. If you condemn Britain, the Ottoman Empire and Germany will be happy, but Italy will be angry. Condemning France will please Romania and the Ottomans.

Bulgaria is currently angry with you. What should you do to maintain your alliance's unity?

PUZZLE 37

Can you insert the letters Z, O, N, E, S into the grid so that each letter only occurs once in each row, each column and each of the five shaded zones?

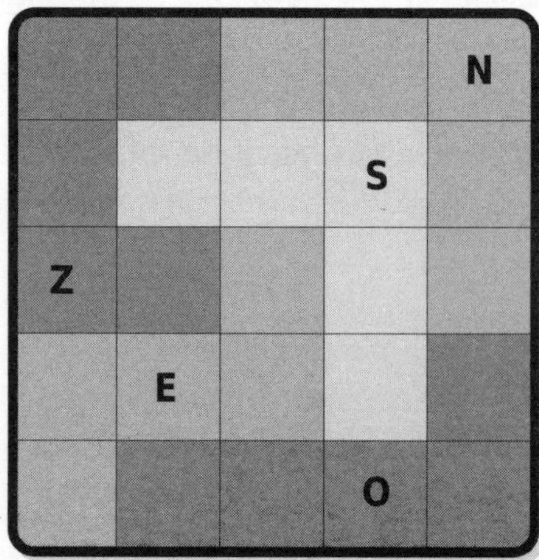

PUZZLE 38

Each letter of the alphabet has been encrypted to a number (1 to 26). Crack the code to solve the puzzle and reveal a number of words that could be related to the Great War, along with others that are not. To start you off, the codes for three letters have been given.

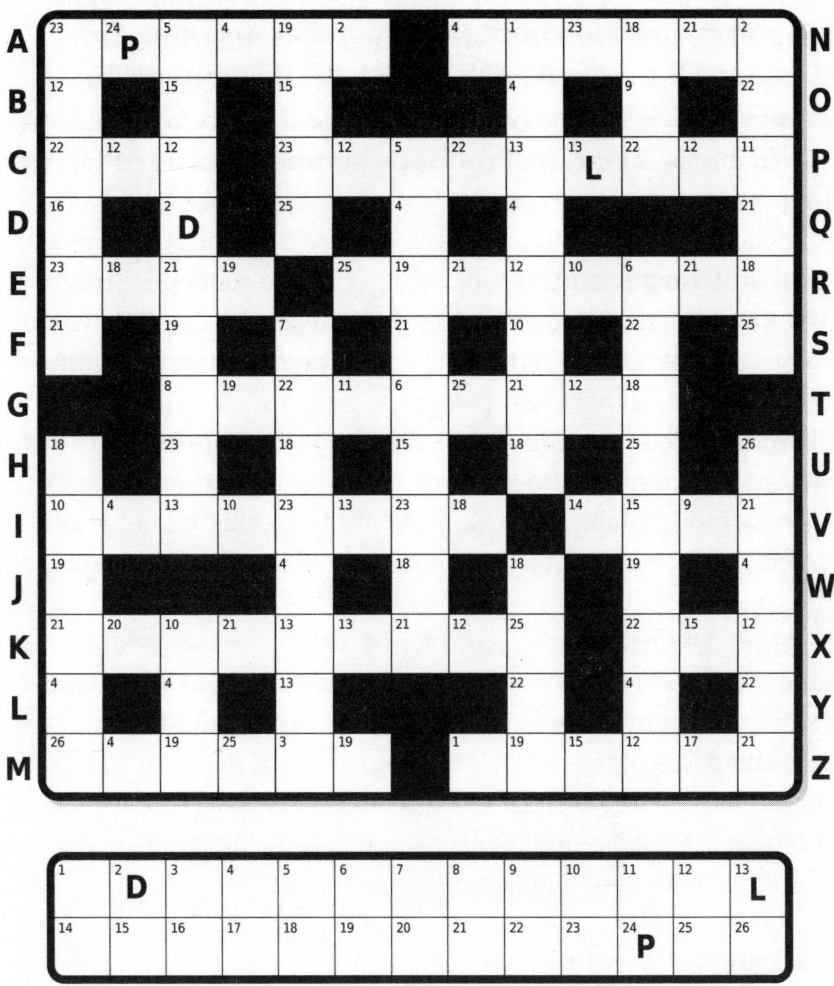

1	2 D	3	4	5	6	7	8	9	10	11	12	13 L
14	15	16	17	18	19	20	21	22	23	24 P	25	26

SOLUTIONS PAGE 187-8

AMBITIONS

At the start of the twentieth century, Europe was in a state of political flux. This was not a novel situation – the continent's empires and kingdoms had been jostling for power and contending with popular uprisings for centuries. But even Napoleon's colossal ambitions for France during the early nineteenth century could not start the first *world* war; that dubious honour would not fall to just one man or one nation.

Russian Imperialism

The Russian Empire covered a sixth of the world's land mass and, with a population of 128 million, could mobilise a larger army than any of the other great powers. It was, however, lagging behind both economically and technologically. After a century of successful conquests, Russia's fortunes started to change for the worse – most notably in its capitulation to an alliance of various powers at the end of the Crimean War (1856) and a humiliating defeat at the hands of the Japanese in 1905.

Russia saw itself as the protector of Europe's Slavic people. Its failure to prevent Austria-Hungary from taking Slavic Bosnia from the Ottoman Empire in 1908 represented both a loss of face and a loss of territorial advantage in the Balkans. If Russia wanted to reassert itself as an imperial power, it would need to do so on the Balkan Peninsula, even if that meant entering into hostilities with neighbouring empires.

Balkan Nationalism

The concept of nationalism emerged and strengthened throughout the nineteenth century. In the Balkans, this caused great instability in the Ottoman Empire, as Christians – whose rights were restricted in comparison to Muslims – began to demand autonomy. A series of armed revolts led eventually to the Congress of Berlin in 1878, in which the boundaries of newly independent and semi-independent Balkan nations were set.

The young nations began to create alliances of their own. Serbian nationalism surged, along with pro-Russia sentiment. When Serbia and Bulgaria announced a joint customs union in 1905, neighbouring Austria-Hungary responded with an embargo aimed at damaging the burgeoning Serbian economy.

Bosnia's independence was curtailed by Austria-Hungarian administration over it. This limited independence was erased when it was annexed by Austria-Hungary in 1908. Serbia saw this as a provocation and war was only narrowly avoided.

In 1912, the Balkan League (Greece, Serbia, Bulgaria and Montenegro) declared war on the Ottoman Empire. The League's victory resulted in substantial territorial gains, particularly for Greece and Serbia. Bulgaria felt short-changed, so it made war on its former allies – a doomed endeavour which permitted the Ottoman Empire to re-enter the fray and resulted in the Treaty of Bucharest (1913). A triumphant Serbia doubled the size of its territory, while a defeated Bulgaria turned to Austria-Hungary for support. Serbo-Austrian relations reached an all-time low.

PUZZLE 39

What comes next in this Morse code sequence?

And, from your knowledge of the First World War, what is the connection between this puzzle and Alfred Graf von Schlieffen?

•
▬ ▬ • •
▬ • •
• • • ▬
• • ▬ •
• • •
• • •
• ▬
▬ •
▬ ▬ • •
•
....

SOLUTIONS PAGE 188

PUZZLE 40

The numbers have been replaced by the letters **DEILNPRSZ** in this Sudoku. Can you solve it to reveal the word in the shaded boxes?

	R	N			D			
		L		Z				
I	D		N	S				
	S					L		D
L								R
P		Z					S	
				N	S		L	P
				D		E		
			Z			D	R	

PUZZLE 41

Can you complete the message below by writing a number in letters to ensure that the content is true?

Yesterday our cryptology department decrypted this message and we can confirm that the letter R occurs__________times. No further action is required.

ASSASSINATION

The murder of heads of state was not uncommon in the nineteenth century. An assassination might result in a regime change but could also provoke swells of support for the affected government or monarchy.

In the Balkans, revolutionary secret societies had been formed with the aim of liberating Serbs and Slavs in occupied countries. Two such groups were Young Bosnia, which was mostly comprised of student activists, and the Black Hand, which drew its members from the Serbian military. Both saw violence as a justifiable means to achieve their goals.

The shot heard around the world

On 28 June 1914, Archduke Franz Ferdinand, heir to the Austro-Hungarian throne, and his wife Sophie visited the city of Sarajevo in Bosnia. At least six members of Young Bosnia planned to assassinate the Archduke as he travelled through the city in an open-topped car. Their plot initially backfired: a timed explosive detonated under another vehicle in the motorcade, injuring twenty members of the entourage but leaving the Archduke unharmed, and unperturbed.

Ferdinand continued with his duties. He attended a town hall reception and then decided to visit the hospital where the bomb victims were being treated. One of the would-be assassins, Gavrilo Princip, happened to still be on the chosen route and seized his opportunity. He shot the Archduke and his wife at close range, killing them both.

Who was Archduke Franz Ferdinand?

Franz Ferdinand was not a popular man. Despite being heir to the throne, he was ostracised by members of the royal household because his wife did not have royal blood. He also showed open contempt for non-Austrians, in particular Hungarians, making him few friends at home or abroad.

SOLUTIONS PAGE 189

Initially, his death did not prompt much outrage from the nations of Europe who had become accustomed to violence in the Balkans. However, Ferdinand could be described as politically moderate by the standards of his time. He fervently opposed going to war with Russia and wanted to promote a more federalist structure within the empire itself, potentially giving the various constituent parts more autonomy than they currently had. But with his death, more belligerent voices came to the fore. They were determined to use his assassination as a *casus belli* against Serbia.

Who was Gavrilo Princip?

A fervent nationalist and a member of the Young Bosnians, Princip had resolved to kill the Archduke when he announced his planned visit to Bosnia three months earlier. Immediately after the assassination, Princip tried to commit suicide, but the pistol was wrestled from his hand and he was arrested. At 19 years of age, he was too young to receive the death penalty, so he was sentenced to 27 years in prison instead. He died of tuberculosis less than four years later.

Princip and his comrades had allegedly visited Serbia where they were given arms and training by the Black Hand. The involvement of this secret society is a critical piece in the 'Great War' puzzle – it allowed Austria-Hungary to blame the nation of Serbia rather than just a separatist group for the death of their Archduke.

PUZZLE 42

Decrypt this message:

E BJ B YUCLRHBV KBTELKBHERT BEJEKC ALQ TDI UKEAESBTELK LA BHH YUCLRHBVR BKN E NL KLT SBQI WDBT ALQJ LA RTBTI OUT ET JURT OI AQIIN AQLJ BURTQEB

Clue (Atbash): GSV PVBDLIW RH Z YZOPZM XLFMGIB GSZG BVZIMH GL YV UIVV

PUZZLE 43

Shade the cells so that each number represents the total number of shaded cells touching that cell, including diagonally, and including itself. What two words are revealed?

	5	4					5		4		5	3	2	
4					6	4		4		5	8	5		
3	6	3		3		3	6		6			4		
			6	3		4	7	4		5				0
		2							4				1	
3		3	4		5	4	5			2	4	2		1
3				3			3			2	4			
5	7	4			6					2		2		1
				4	4	1	2				4			
4	7			5			2	1	3	2			1	
			4		4	2	3			2				
	3		2			2		2	4				1	
	0						2	2			3			
					0			2			2			
	0			0			1		2				0	

SOLUTIONS PAGE 189-90

PUZZLE 44

Each letter of the alphabet has been encrypted to a number (1 to 26). Can you fill the grid below with words to work out the code? Solve the clue first, and you will see that all the words are connected.

Clue (Atbash): GSV OLMTVHG DLIW RH GSV XZKRGZO LU GSV LGGLNZM VNKRIV

1	2	3	4	5	6	7	8	9	10	11	12	13
14	15	16	17	18	19	20	21	22	23	24	25	26

THE JULY CRISIS

The assassination of Archduke Franz Ferdinand was followed by a series of portentous events throughout the month of July 1914. This is the point where the cause of the war becomes contentious. Clearly there was a breakdown of diplomacy – but who was to blame?

At his trial, Gavrilo Princip insisted that the Serbian state (via the Black Hand) had not been involved in planning the assassination, but this was angrily dismissed by the Austro-Hungarian government. The Austrians were eager to take reprisals against Serbia and made it known that support for Bosnian nationalism would come at a heavy cost. The Hungarians were opposed to this course of action, however, and even the most hawkish Austrians knew that it would be impossible to act against Serbia without angering its gargantuan ally: Russia.

The Austro-Hungarian government petitioned their neighbour, the German Empire, to come to their aid in the event that Russia reacted with force. Germany not only agreed but encouraged the Austro-Hungarians to act quickly while international public opinion was still hostile towards Serbia. Germany's monarch Kaiser Wilhelm and his chief of staff Helmuth von Moltke saw this as an opportunity: strike Russia before it had time to bring its formidable war machine to bear along with those of its allies France and Britain.

Having made this decision, Kaiser Wilhelm decided to take a holiday – a cruise to Norway! Some believe that this gesture at a time of international emergency was a calculated manoeuvre. On 23 July 1914, the Serbian government received Austria-Hungary's ultimatum. It consisted of ten demands, worded in such a way as to cause maximum humiliation to Serbia if it acquiesced. Serbia was given 48 hours to comply. A British attempt to mediate was rejected by Austria-Hungary and Germany.

SOLUTIONS PAGE 190

PUZZLE 45

Here is a quote from Britain's First Lord of the Admiralty regarding the ultimatum. Can you decrypt it?

VOYDQZBTYUVFVPALZNWTYE
VVNTEURCEFLDPCFLPZULL

Clue (Atbash): ZM RGZORZM XRKSVI ZMW Z UFGFIV YIRGRHS KIRNV NRMRHGVI

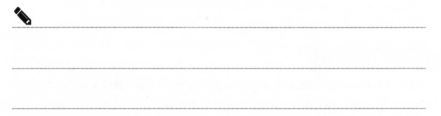

Serbia immediately consulted its ally, Russia. The Russians could see the ultimatum was a provocation, but they were not yet ready to commit to entering into a war.

Just before the deadline was about to expire, Serbia gave its response. It agreed to almost all the demands, promising to condemn Serbian nationalist groups and anti-Austrian propaganda, but it could not sanction an investigation by Austro-Hungarian officials on Serbian soil. No one had expected this abject surrender of sovereignty to be complied with, and Austria-Hungary took the aggregate response to its ultimatum to be 'No'.

On 28 July, one month to the day since the assassination, Austria-Hungary declared war on Serbia. In response, Russia declared war on Austria-Hungary, and, on 1 August, Germany declared war on Russia and France. It proceeded to attack the latter by advancing through neutral Belgium. Britain responded to this blatant aggression by declaring war on Germany.

The First World War had begun.

PUZZLE 46

A diplomat has a peculiar set of opinions.
He likes Ottomans but not Austrians.
He likes Bosnians but not Serbs.
He likes Macedonians but not Greeks.
He likes Gaul but not France.
He likes Italy but hates the Mediterranean.

Does he like Russians?

PUZZLE 47

Here is a house of cards, three storeys high, which consists of 15 cards. If you had the dexterity and a standard deck of 52 cards, how many storeys could you construct using the same method?

SOLUTIONS PAGE 190-1

PUZZLE 48

This is a shifty puzzle. Can you decrypt and determine which of the statements are true?

1. BMM PG UIPTF CFMPX BSF USVF
2. PQPG QH VJQUG DGNQY CTG VTWG
3. RQH RI WKRVH DERYH LV WUXH
4. EPP SJ XLSWI EFSZI EVI XVYI
5. STSJ TK YMTXJ FGTAJ NX YWZJ
6. GRR UL ZNUYK GHUBK GXK LGRYK

PUZZLE 49

Can you find five words relating to the First World War hidden in the following lines? For example, the word 'war' is hidden in the phrase 'how are the troops?'. One word is hidden in each line.

1. Hidden behind a wall, I edged closer to the enemy.
2. The morning briefing was an anticlimax; I sensed they had run out of ideas.
3. I saw, flying towards the town centre, a type of aircraft I'd never seen before.
4. Weather conditions felt almost polar; mist, ice and blizzards made for very cold nights on the Western Front.
5. A hot meal could help to break the tedium, or a letter from home – that was very special indeed.

SIGNING UP

At the beginning of the war, Great Britain had almost a quarter of a million regular troops, backed up by 200,000 reservists and 250,000 Territorials. But a significant number of the regular troops were stationed in the overseas colonies and could not be immediately deployed to Europe.

Britain was proud of its well-trained standing army and did not believe in forced conscription. This reliance on quality over quantity, however, meant its army was massively outnumbered by the German Empire, which could field 98 infantry divisions compared to Britain's six. German soldiers were also well trained and disciplined, although they failed to seize a hoped-for quick victory on the continent against France and Russia's large armies.

Britain's Secretary of State for War, Lord Kitchener, asked for volunteers to make up the deficit. His famous recruitment campaign began on 7 August 1914 and called on men aged between 18 and 30 and at least 5 feet 6 inches in height to sign up. The age, height and health requirements changed at points as the war progressed to help fill the ranks. By the end of August, 30,000 volunteers were answering the call each day, and by the end of the war over 2.5 million British men had volunteered.

PUZZLE 50

On 7 August 1914, Sergeant Enfield's oldest son Henry is twice as old as his younger brother Mark and half as old as his father. In 20 years, Mark will be half his father's age. **Is Henry old enough to volunteer?**

SOLUTIONS PAGE 191-2

WOMEN AT WAR

With so many men leaving to serve in the armed forces, there was a shortage of labour on the home front. Britain looked to its female population to replenish the workforce. Many women were employed in the new munitions factories, a demanding and potentially dangerous occupation but essential for the war effort. Others took on roles that had been previously occupied by men, such as police officers, firefighters, postal workers and bank clerks. They were paid less than their male counterparts, and it was expected that they would stand down when the war ended.

OBJECTION

Despite a surge in patriotic fervour, not everyone was keen to go to war. Around 16,000 British men registered as conscientious objectors, citing religious or moral grounds against the use of military force. Although some of these men were reallocated to non-combat duties, those who refused to participate in any way were imprisoned and subjected to harsh treatment. Some women took to publicly approaching men not wearing uniform and presenting them with a white feather as a symbol of cowardice.

DESPERATE MEASURES

Initially it was easy to fill the ranks, especially after the creation of 'Pals Battalions', which allowed men to serve alongside their friends, neighbours or work colleagues in units with a distinct identity. This proved popular but also meant that some communities and families lost many of their young men during intense fighting in which these units were involved.

The requirements to sign up became less restrictive as time went on: by 1918 the maximum recruitment age was raised to 51 and the height requirement had dropped to 5 feet 3 inches. The Army High Command had become so desperate for new recruits that they formally adopted compulsory military service – conscription – in 1916. By the end of the war, more than 5 million men had served in Britain's army

PUZZLE 51

Lieutenant Smith had joined the Corps of Royal Engineers and was reporting to his commanding officer, Captain Jones.

Captain Jones lit his pipe with a Swan Vesta, blew out the match and laid it carefully on his desk. Smith noticed that there were five other identical matches on the desk.

'Test of technical competence, Smith,' said the CO. *'I want you to make four equilateral triangles out of these six matches, without breaking any of them.'*

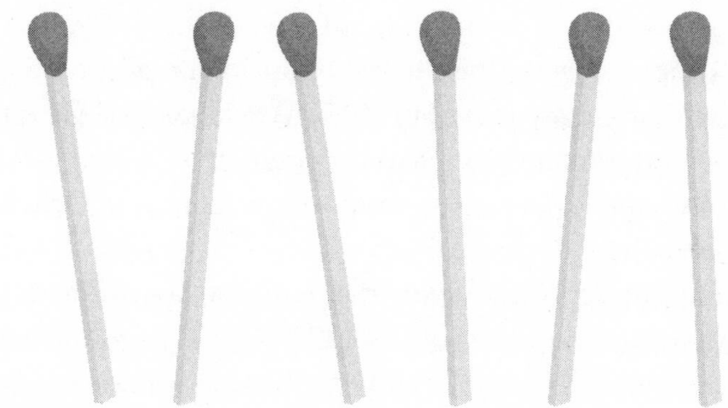

TAKING SIDES (PART I)

Initially, the 'Great War' appeared to be a clash between the nations of the Triple Entente and those of the Triple Alliance. But as new belligerents joined the fray, the opposing contingents expanded and the conflict became global.

THE CENTRAL POWERS

Although Italy had been part of the Triple Alliance, it declared itself neutral at the outbreak of war since it had not signed up to pursuing a war of aggression. The Ottoman Empire was more than happy to join the German Empire and Austria-Hungary in 1914 as the Central Powers (named as such owing to their location sandwiched between France and Russia). The Kingdom of Bulgaria, still seething from its defeat in the Second Balkan War, sided with the powers a year later.

SOLUTIONS PAGE 192

THE ALLIES

On 4 September 1914, the members of the Triple Entente agreed not to pursue separate peace deals from each other. Subsequently, they became known as the Allies. Great Britain's involvement brought soldiers not only from the British Isles but from its overseas Dominion, colonies and territories, including Australia, New Zealand, Canada, India, parts of Africa and the Caribbean. The Russian Empire also included Finland and part of Poland, and the French army included colonial troops from North and West Africa, as well as Indo-China (Vietnam today).

Japan joined the Allies in 1914, but it was more interested in expanding its own empire than honouring its pact with the British. Similarly, Italy joined in 1915 in exchange for the return of its 'lost' Austrian territories in the event of an Allied victory. A host of other nations began to support the Allies too, including Brazil, Greece and Romania.

Russia underwent seismic turmoil with the overthrow of its monarchy and two revolutions in 1917. The new Bolshevik government signed an armistice with the Central Powers in December. In April of the same year, the United States, angered by submarine attacks on its merchant vessels in the Atlantic, declared war on Germany.

PUZZLE 52

Complete the sequence:

77	49	36	18	....

PUZZLE 53

Place a mine into some of the empty cells so that each number represents the total count of mines in neighbouring cells, including diagonally adjacent cells.

	2		2				1	
		2		1	1	1		
2		3	2			2		2
2				1			3	
	4		3		2		4	
	3			1				2
1		1			1	3		3
		2	3	2		3		
	2				1		3	

A NEW KIND OF WAR

In August 1914, many nations went into the war in the belief that it would be fought in a manner similar to earlier conflicts, where lines of men advanced on the enemy, with the advantage lying with the attacker.

They quickly learned that innovations such as quick-firing artillery, machine guns and magazine-loading rifles fundamentally altered how violence was perpetuated on the battlefield. The advantage was with the defender. Technology, tactics and world politics had entered a new era.

SOLUTIONS PAGE 192-3

PUZZLE 54

At the start of the war, the headgear issued to British soldiers was a simple cap made of cloth. The number of casualties resulting from head injuries became a matter of great concern to the War Office, so it replaced cloth caps with steel helmets.

Alarmingly, after the introduction of the helmet, some field hospitals reported that the number of soldiers treated for head injuries had *increased*. **Why might this be?**

BREAKING THE RULES

The Hague Conventions of 1899 and 1907 were international treaties aimed at regulating the conduct of warring nations. They prescribed acceptable treatment of prisoners and civilians and what types of weapons should be prohibited in an armed conflict.

Many of these rules were ignored from the start. Germany's invasion of Belgium violated a convention which forbade a nation attacking another without prior warning. Another rule prohibited the use of poison as a weapon but both sides employed poison gas throughout the war. The war also saw the start of aerial bombing, which ostensibly targeted enemy industrial production and transport but caused civilian casualties as well, something the Hague Conventions had sought to prevent.

SPYING AND SUBVERSION

Although espionage had been an essential part of statecraft and strategy for hundreds of years, the nineteenth century saw the birth of national military intelligence agencies. By the outbreak of the 'Great War', espionage had become increasingly sophisticated, and what we now regard as the archetypal 'spy' entered the public imagination.

Information on enemy plans and capabilities could be obtained most effectively by spy networks in enemy territory. The mistreatment of local people by the Germans in occupied Belgium, northern France and Luxembourg prompted many to volunteer as spies for the Allies, which gave them an advantage.

Germany's network of spies was smaller and less effective than the Allies' but did boast two remarkable female spies: Elsbeth Schragmüller, who was awarded the Iron Cross First Class for heading the *Kriegsnachrichtenstelle* (an intelligence bureau directed against France and Great Britain) in Antwerp; and the less fortunate Margaretha Geertruida Zelle, a Dutch exotic dancer who was executed by a French firing squad and was better known by her stage name Mata Hari. In 1915, two years before Mata Hari's execution, the Germans had shot British nurse Edith Cavell on a charge of treason for helping Allied soldiers escape occupied Belgium.

A British archaeologist, Thomas Edward Lawrence, joined the British Army as a volunteer in 1914 and was deployed to the Middle East on an intelligence mission two years later. The Allies' objective was to break up the Ottoman Empire by lending support to an Arab uprising. This was ultimately successful (at least from a British point of view) and Lawrence's participation, both diplomatic and in combat, gave him international recognition as 'Lawrence of Arabia'.

PUZZLE 55

Can you decrypt the following using brute force?

RK RCYQY D RSNJ DJ RCYQY D RNSQR
ONKRCYN HYPT PJT QDQRYN QRYYH
RK CDQ OHDJT LKVYN D IPGY PLLYPH
D BSPNT CYN OYPSRX EHYPJ ANKI NSQR

CY QLDJQ PJT OSNJQ PJT HKUYQ RCY PDN
PJT QLHDRQ P QGSHH RK VDJ IX LNPDQY
OSR SL RCY JKOHX IPNECDJB TPXQ
QCY BHDRRYNQ JPGYT EKHT PJT APDN

QVYYR QDQRYN BNPJR XKSN QKHTDYN RCDQ
RCPR DJ BKKT ASNX CY IPX AYYH
RCY OKTX VCYNY CY QYRQ CDQ CYYH
MSPDH ANKI XKSN TKVJVPNT TPNRDJB GDQQ

Clue (Atbash): KLVGIB

SOLUTIONS PAGE 193

THE WAR ON LAND

At the start of the war, Germany did not want to divide its strength by fighting on two fronts simultaneously. The Germans believed that if they quickly overran France, they could then turn their full military strength against Russia. This plan quickly faced a series of setbacks which took the war in a different direction and ensured that it would not be over swiftly.

TRENCHES

Firepower had advanced considerably since the debut of the Gatling gun in the American Civil War. As guns improved their range, penetration and rate of fire, infantry could no longer hope to prevail by simply standing their ground. Troops advancing in the open stood no chance against entrenched defenders armed with machine guns and formidable artillery. As a result, over a million men had been killed by the end of 1914. The most obvious solution was to dig in and take up defensive positions. A stalemate ensued. This deadlock meant living in trench networks where artillery bombardments, machine gun fire, the threat of poison gas, limited sanitation, an abundance of rats and lice and the spread of disease combined to make life difficult and dangerous. Maintaining morale was a constant challenge, and some soldiers became mentally ill as a result of the strain.

On the Western Front, trenches stretched from the North Sea coast deep into France and to the Swiss frontier. Almost 2,500 kilometres of trenches were dug during the conflict and neither side gained much ground during the middle years of the war. Although they were not a new feature in war, trenches are now closely associated with the 'Great War' and the difficult conditions in which it was fought on the Western Front.

PUZZLE 56

You must navigate a course from the east trench to the west trench, moving from one square to the next, either horizontally or vertically but not diagonally. You can only move from an A square to a B, from a B to a C, from a C to a D and from a D to an A. **Where do you start and finish?**

East

B	D	C	D	B	D	A	D	A	B	C	B
A	C	B	A	D	C	B	C	D	A	D	A
A	B	A	D	C	B	D	B	A	B	C	A
B	C	D	B	D	A	D	B	D	C	D	B
C	D	A	D	C	B	A	D	A	B	C	A
A	B	C	A	D	C	D	B	D	C	B	C
D	A	B	D	C	D	C	A	C	D	A	D
B	C	D	A	B	A	B	C	D	A	B	A
C	A	A	C	D	A	C	A	C	D	A	B

West

PUZZLE 57

It takes six French soldiers six hours to dig six metres of trench. Four British soldiers can dig four metres of trench in four hours. A combined taskforce of twelve French soldiers and twelve British soldiers are given twelve hours to dig a trench. How many metres of trench can they dig?

SOLUTIONS PAGE 194

LAND BATTLES

MARNE (1ST BATTLE)
5–12 September 1914

The war began on the Western Front with a German advance through Belgium into France and the British Expeditionary Force and the French Fifth Army's withdrawal (which came to be known as 'the Great Retreat'). The Germans were so confident of success that they decided to bypass the French capital in order to pursue their enemies. But on the banks of the River Marne, some ten miles from Paris, the Allies launched a counter-attack.

During the battle, the exhausted French and British troops did not just hold their ground but forced the Germans into a retreat. However, casualties were high on both sides. The ensuing breakdown of communications and problems with supplies forced the Germans to withdraw and regroup.

Both sides were desperate to gain an advantage and a succession of outflanking manoeuvres that became known as the 'Race to the Sea' followed. This too was indecisive. The combatants started digging defensive trenches and the Western Front stagnated into a war of attrition.

YPRES (2ND BATTLE)
22 April–25 May 1915

Near the Flemish town of Ypres in western Belgium, the German army used chlorine gas as a weapon for the first time on the Western Front. The first troops to suffer from the use of this weapon were French territorial and colonial troops This insidious form of attack caused severe breathing problems, and the very threat of poison gas took a psychological toll too.

The head of the Canadian Expeditionary Force's field laboratory, Dr George Nasmith, realised that chlorine gas could be countered by ammonia and advised troops to cover their faces with cloth drenched in their own urine. Although they were pushed back, the Canadians would not cede the town. The fighting continued without a breakthrough, and Ypres was devastated by German artillery fire.

VERDUN
21 February–18 December 1916

A German artillery shell hitting the cathedral in the French town of Verdun-sur-Meuse signalled the start of the longest battle of the 'Great War'. The subsequent bombardment of the town lasted for 10 hours and was followed by a series of brutal assaults and counterattacks that went on for another 302 days.

Both sides suffered almost half a million casualties, making it one of the costliest battles in history. The French were ultimately victorious, having defended their position, but the losses they sustained had a devastating impact on national morale and hampered the French Army's ability to launch a counter-offensive.

GALLIPOLI
25 April 1915–9 January 1916

In the east, the Allies embarked upon a campaign intended to allow Allied shipping to pass through the Dardanelles to assist Russia, and take the Ottoman Empire out of the war by capturing its capital, Constantinople. Alongside British, Indian, Irish and French units, a significant number of troops assigned to this operation were from the Australian and New Zealand Army Corps (ANZAC).

Unfortunately, Allied Command had underestimated both the resolve of the defenders and the effects of the environment. After initial failed naval attacks occurring in March 1915, the Ottomans held the landing forces at their beachheads and fighting stagnated into all-too-familiar trench warfare. The blistering summer heat, accompanied by swarms of flies and outbreaks of sickness, tested the attackers' endurance to breaking point. Although the Allies were ultimately forced to evacuate and withdraw, Gallipoli is often associated with the camaraderie of the ANZACs, and is viewed by many in Australia and New Zealand as the coming of age of their nations.

SOMME
1 July–18 November 1916

On the Western Front, the Allies were determined to break the stalemate with an all-out attack. The French Army was exhausted and depleted after their defence of Verdun, so this operation was led by the British and its various imperial forces. Many of the volunteers who had joined up in the war's early months had their first experience of fighting during the Battle of the Somme.

An opening seven-day artillery bombardment did little to weaken the German's meticulously constructed defences, and the British infantry marched into a bloodbath, with 19,240 men dead on the first day alone. After five months of attritional, bloody fighting, total casualties including all sides exceeded one million. The Somme became a defining battle of the war, both in terms of its human cost and the later improvements made by the British in the use of artillery and infantry tactics that affected the war's ultimate outcome.

PASSCHENDAELE (3RD BATTLE OF YPRES)
31 July–10 November 1917

The third major engagement fought in Ypres was a British-led offensive towards the rural village of Passchendaele. The primary objective was to capture the strategically important railway hub of Roulers. A distinguishing feature of the battle was the effect of the weather.

Torrential rainfall before and during the battle turned the cratered ground into a swamp of debris, corpses and churned-up mud. This quagmire made the use of horse-drawn transport and tanks almost impossible. The fighting was bloody, with the loss of over a quarter of a million men. Once again, the deadlock on the Western Front remained and the village of Passchendaele was razed to the ground.

AMIENS
8–12 August 1918

In spring 1918, it seemed the Germans had gained a decisive upper hand with a series of offensives that deployed elite assault troops and rained down very accurate artillery fire to batter the Allies. Despite being forced to retreat, the Allies hung on and were able to launch a counter-attack at Amiens in August 1918. The Allies had learned many harsh lessons over the course of the war, and put that knowledge into practice near the northern French city of Amiens.

Unlike previous battles, which commenced with a ferocious artillery barrage, the Allies began their next major offensive in relative secrecy. Over 500 Allied tanks and around 2000 aircraft combined with British, French, Australian, Canadian, and American infantry divisions to deliver a highly successful surprise attack. The Allies gained over seven miles of ground on the first day.

Allied casualties at the battle were around 44,000, compared to the 75,000 sustained by the Germans, many of whom surrendered. General Erich Ludendorff called it 'the black day of the German Army.' The end of the war was finally in sight.

PUZZLE 58

Each letter of the alphabet has been encrypted to a number (1 to 26). Crack the code to solve the puzzle and reveal a long vertically written word that shaped the course of the war. To start you off, the codes for three letters have been given.

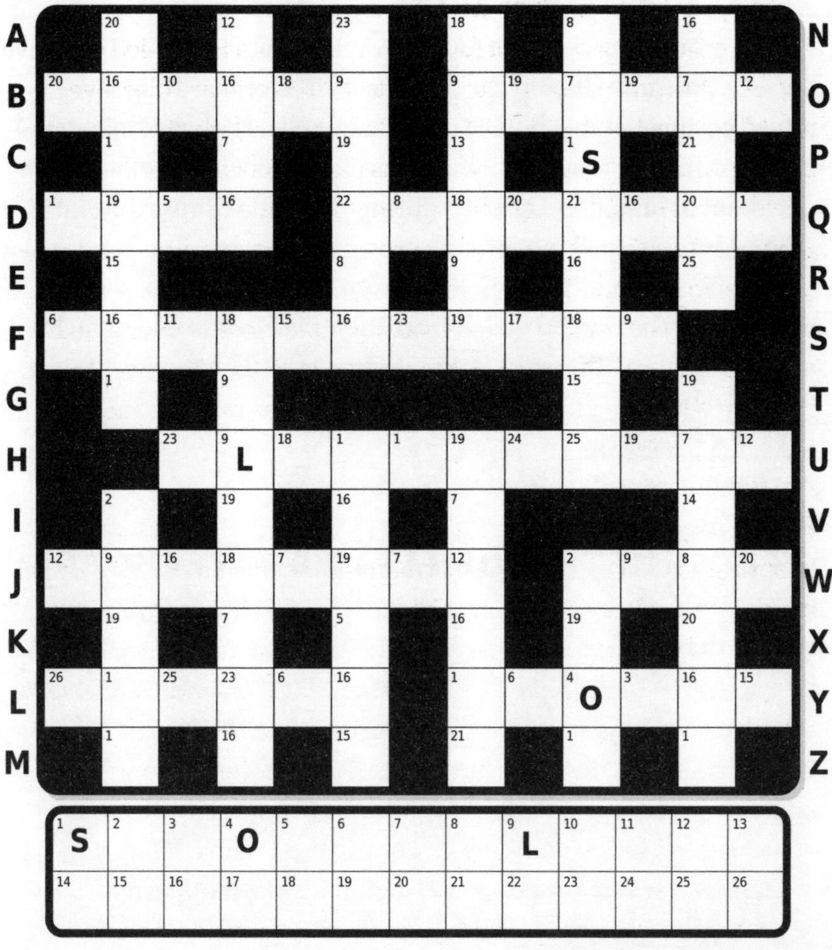

SOLUTIONS PAGE 195

TANKS!

How do you assault an entrenched enemy while simultaneously protecting your own troops? The solution now seems obvious (it had occurred to Leonardo da Vinci back in 1487), but it was not until the latter half of the 'Great War' that armoured fighting vehicles were incorporated into tactics used by ground combat forces.

The first tank to see service was the British Mark I. It was armoured to withstand machine gun fire, equipped with tracked wheels to crush barbed wire and had a distinctive rhomboid hull so it could cross trenches. It was armed with two 6-pounder guns and/or a brace of machine guns, and its maximum speed was six kilometres per hour.

The Mark I was unleashed on 15 September 1916. Although its appearance shocked the Germans, its debut at the Battle of Flers–Courcelette during the Somme offensive was anticlimactic, in part because of mechanical failure but also because there were too few of the vehicles to make a real difference. However, British Commander-in-Chief Douglas Haig saw their potential and put in an order for 1,000 more tanks.

Work began on improving the design of the Mark I, and other warring nations started developing their own armoured vehicles. It was clear that the future of land warfare would include the tank.

PUZZLE 59

Can you decrypt the question and answer it?

REETENMETNIMORSATAWDHKTEFHOEGS?

Clue (Atbash): GZMPH

PUZZLE 60

Trench Masyu! Draw a continuous line through all the squares that contain bunkers and barbed wire. The line must never cross over itself.

When the line enters a **bunker square**, it must go straight through that square and must turn 90 degrees in the next and/or previous square.

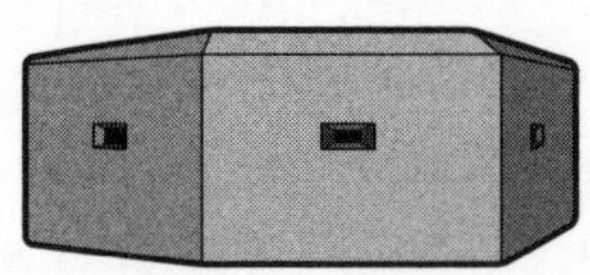

When the line enters a **barbed wire square**, it must turn 90 degrees in that square and must go straight through the next and previous square.

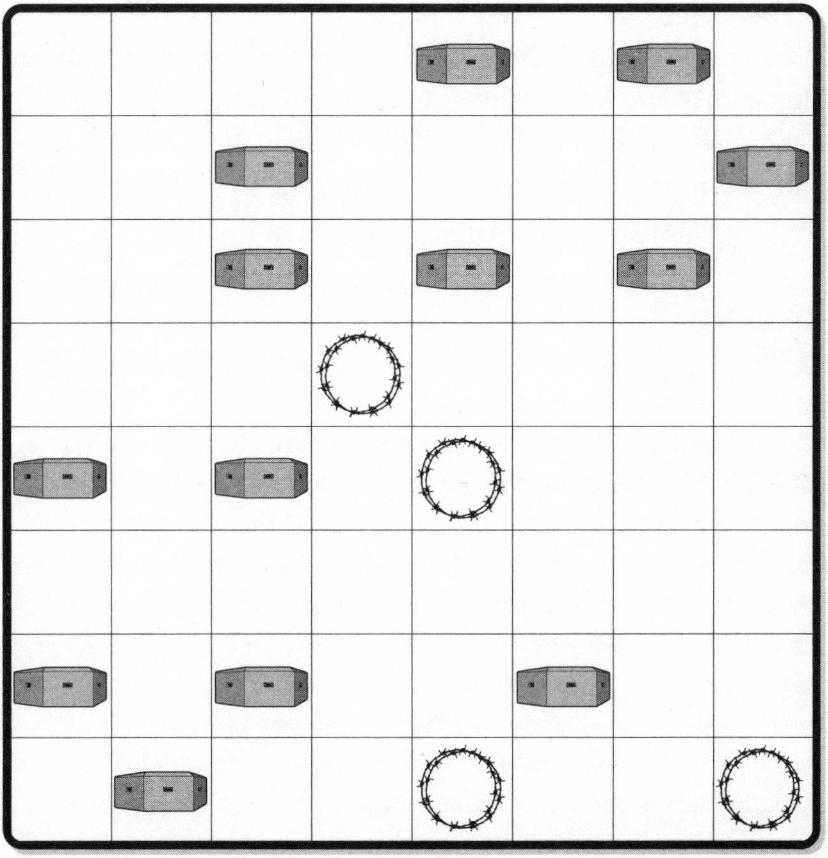

SOLUTIONS PAGE 196

THE WAR AT SEA

Naval warfare during the 'Great War' mostly consisted of blockades and raiding. Both Germany and especially Britain depended on maritime imports to feed their populations and supply their war efforts. Each realised that restricting their enemy's supplies was the key to crippling their ability to wage war. The Royal Navy imposed a blockade which contributed to the Allies' ultimate victory and continued after the war had ended.

Germany was unable to respond with a successful blockade of its own using surface warships, so it turned to raiding by cruisers and armed merchant ships and attacks by its submarine force to hunt and sink Allied merchant vessels.

There were very few naval battles during the First World War. The German High Seas Fleet aimed to destroy significant elements of the Royal Navy's Grand Fleet before fighting a major battle in the North Sea. This strategy ultimately failed and one attempt to achieve this result in 1916 led to a clash of the two battle fleets known as the Battle of Jutland.

JUTLAND

On 31 May 1916, the two nations pitted their fleets against one another. Vice-Admiral Reinhard Scheer commanded the German Navy's High Seas Fleet. He understood that the Royal Navy had a numerical advantage, so he planned an ambush. He hoped to divide the Royal Navy's Grand Fleet, destroy the Battle Cruiser Force under Admiral Sir David Beatty and then lure the Grand Fleet into a trap when it came to assist. However, thanks to Allied code-breakers, the British were forewarned. Although Beatty's force was attacked and forced to withdraw, the Grand Fleet responded sooner than Scheer had anticipated. Britain lost 14 warships, including three battle cruisers, in the engagement, while Germany lost 11 ships, including one battle cruiser. Although the battle appeared inconclusive, German claims of victory were quickly shown as hollow as the High Seas Fleet had failed to significantly dent the power of the Grand Fleet, and never challenged the Royal Navy's control of the North Sea again.

PUZZLE 61

Find the enemy fleet on the grid below. The numbers on the periphery tell you how many occupied squares are in that row or column. No two vessels occupy neighbouring squares (including diagonals). Xs mark empty squares. There are four kinds of vessel, and the number of each in the fleet is as follows:

Battleship ◀■■▶ x1
Cruiser ◀■▶ x2
Destroyer ◀▶ x3
Submarine ■ x4

	3	1	2	4	2	2	1	3	1	1	
7		X	■	X							7
0											0
2											2
3											3
1								■			1
3				◀							3
0											0
4											4
0											0
0											0
	3	1	2	4	2	2	1	3	1	1	

SOLUTIONS PAGE 196

THE WAR IN THE AIR

Aerial warfare had limited potential at the start of the 'Great War' because aircraft were in their infancy. Balloons had been employed by the military as far back as the French Revolutionary Wars (1792–1802) but their role was principally reconnaissance. Balloons and airships were used for observation and artillery spotting in the First World War, but German airships were also the first aircraft used for sustained aerial bombing attacks, with bombing raids on British towns and cities beginning in 1915.

The first heavier-than-air powered aircraft was the Wright Flyer, which had its maiden flight in 1903. The First Balkan War (1912) saw aircraft used as primitive bombers for the first time. Shortly after, the British refitted some of their early aircraft for bombing operations. These were used for tactical raids during the early months of the First World War.

In order to counter aerial attacks, artillery was repurposed, but a more dynamic deterrent was on its way as aircraft began to carry machine guns: Dutch aviator Anthony Fokker developed one of the first 'fighters' – aircraft fitted with a machine gun synchronised to fire through the aircraft's propeller.

Fighter pilots became celebrated heroes during the war, most especially the 'Aces'. These were pilots who had shot down at least five enemy aircraft. They included:

Manfred von Richthofen
'The Red Baron'
Germany / Luftstreitkräfte
Rank: Captain
Aerial victories: 80
Awards: Pour le Mérite, Iron Cross First Class, among others

René Fonck
France / Service Aéronautique
Rank: Captain (1918)
Aerial victories: 75
Awards: Légion d'honneur, Croix de Guerre, among others

William Bishop
Canada / Royal Air Force
Rank: Lieutenant (1918)
Aerial victories: 72
Awards: Victoria Cross, Military Cross, among others

Edward Rickenbacker
United States / Army Air Service
Rank: Captain
Aerial victories: 26
Awards: Medal of Honor

Edward 'Mick' Mannock
United Kingdom / Royal Air Force
Rank: Major
Aerial victories: 61
Awards: Victoria Cross, Military Cross, DSO, among others

PUZZLE 62

Which of the boxes (A, B, C or D) completes the grid below?

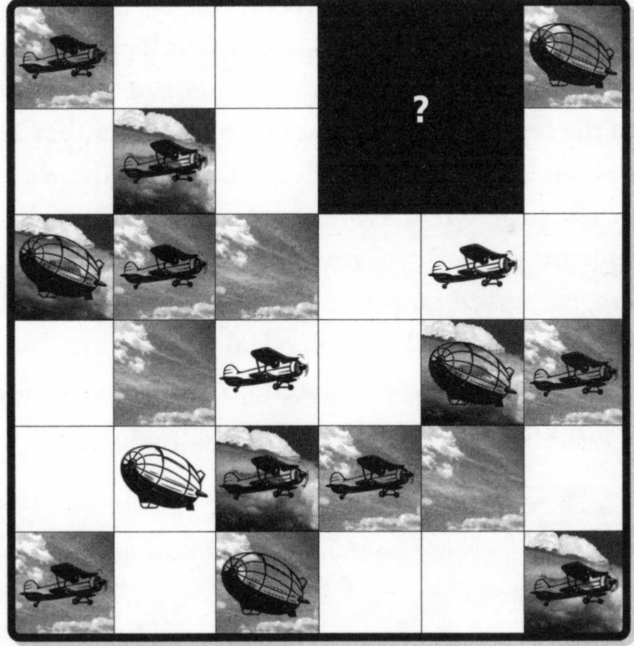

A

B

C

D

SOLUTIONS PAGE 197

THE WAR TO END ALL WARS?

The United States of America joined the war on the Allied side in 1917. It started to send troops to the Western front in large numbers in 1918, which changed the balance of power significantly. The Battle of Amiens was just the start of the Hundred Days Offensive, a rapid undoing of the German gains during the Spring Offensives. Each victory boosted the Allies' resolve and eroded the morale of the Central Powers. There were also Allied successes in the east, such as the Battle of Megiddo (19–25 September 1918), which took the Ottoman Empire out of the war.

Beset by worsening problems with its supply chain to the war fronts, the final nail in the coffin for the German Empire was a revolution, which caused the end of its monarchy. Germany had been battered into submission and formally agreed to the terms of its surrender on 11 November 1918.

At the eleventh hour on the eleventh day of the eleventh month of 1918, the Great War came to an end. What began with pride and patriotic fervour ended with a catastrophic loss of life, collapsed empires, strained economies and enormous psychological and physical destruction. Such were the consequences, few imagined a war on this scale - or worse - could happen again.

PUZZLE 63

How many times per day do the hour and minute hands of a clock cross one another?

PUZZLE 64

Five soldiers are due to be awarded medals for bravery. **Can you work out the surname, rank and regiment of each soldier from the clues below?**

1. Richard Jones was proud to serve in the Infantry; he was not a Major.
2. Corporal Smith was well liked.
3. The Sergeant who served in the Yeomanry was not called Anderson.
4. Henry Barnes did not serve in the Yeomanry and was not a Lieutenant.
5. The Cavalry Lieutenant served with distinction.
6. The soldier who served in the Artillery regiment was not a Corporal.
7. George Webster was not a Private or a member of the Engineers.

Surname	Rank	Regiment

SOLUTIONS PAGE 197

PUZZLE 65

Shade the cells so that each number represents the total number of shaded cells touching that cell, including diagonally, and including itself. What three words are revealed?

3	5	3			5	3	2							0		
4				4						0		0				0
	6	3				4	3					1	1	1		
	4	2			5								1		0	
3			4							2	3	3			3	
		3	4		4		5	3	4			3	4		4	
4				4		5		5		4					7	
3			5	3			7	4					5	3		
	4	1	4						6			3				
2	2			2	4		4	2		2			3	2	4	3
	2			3	5									3	3	
		0	2			3			5		4	3	4	2	1	
	3		3		8	5	6				6			3	2	
	5	2				4		3						3		
	4				5		4	2		2		3	4	2	1	

PUZZLE 66

You have received another encrypted Sudoku. The numbers have been replaced by the letters ACEILMRST. Can you solve it to reveal the word in the shaded boxes?

		L	T				I	C
S								
	T					E		
M				E			T	
T			R		A			L
	S			M				I
		A					M	
								T
R	C				I	A		

SOLUTIONS PAGE 198

CHAPTER 3

THE SECOND WORLD WAR

After the Central Powers surrendered, ending the 'Great War', the international consensus was that such needless and appalling loss of life should never be allowed to happen again.

The president of the United States, Woodrow Wilson, pledged to create a 'new world order' and called for the formation of a League of Nations, dedicated to resolving future disputes by diplomacy rather than bloodshed. However, Wilson's dream was not widely shared; the United States declined to join the League, preferring a return to isolation over being drawn into European power struggles.

Blame for the war was levelled squarely at Germany, and the Allies were determined to punish the nation to ensure it posed no future military threat. The terms of the Treaty of Versailles, were humiliating and economically crippling for Germany. They had to cede territory, massively scale down their armed forces and pay substantial reparations to France, Britain Belgium and Italy.

The Treaty has been seen as a failure on many levels since it did nothing to subdue the German military's aspirations and left the nation feeling resentful and cornered. The German Empire had only recently been replaced by the liberal Weimar Republic, but this beacon of culture and democracy would not shine for long. Hyperinflation began to devastate the economy and a sense of betrayal gripped the nation, directed mainly at the 'cowardly' politicians who had signed the Treaty of Versailles.

A new political movement, National Socialism, took full advantage of this widespread resentment. It promised to restore German pride and punish those who had betrayed the Fatherland. Its focus was on ethnic rather than civic nationalism; it resolved to 'liberate' Germanic people everywhere, including those in the newly created states such as Austria, Czechoslovakia and Poland.

PUZZLE 67

The sum of all the numbers from 1 to 9 is 45.

Can you work out the sum of all the numbers from 1 to 100?

There is a quicker way than simply adding them all up.

PUZZLE 68

Can you complete this Second World War-themed crossword? If you are struggling with some of the answers, reading the rest of this chapter might help.

ACROSS

1 System for detecting aircraft (5)
5 Famous WWII British fighter aircraft, produced by Supermarine (8)
8 System of defensive fortifications along the eastern French border (7,4)
9 Weaponry and ammunition (9)
11 Famous WWII British fighter aircraft, produced by Hawker (9)
13 A person not in the military (8)
14 Location of an international 1935 crisis that discredited the League of Nations (9)

DOWN

2 Location of a major British evacuation in 1940 (7)
3 What the troops leaving 2 down did (7)
4 Spanish dictator from 1939–1975 (6)
6 Fast military aircraft (8)
7 Truce agreement, as in June 1940 between Germany and France (9)
8 Chinese region under Japanese occupation throughout WWII (9)
10 Nazi plan to invade Britain (3,4)
12 Take control of a territory by force (5)

SOLUTIONS PAGE 199

RISE OF THE NAZIS

A decorated lance corporal in the First World War, Austrian-born Adolf Hitler fervently embraced the tenets of National Socialism and became leader of the National Socialist German Workers' (Nazi) Party in 1921. With 2,000 fellow Nazis, he launched a failed coup to overthrow the Weimar government and was subsequently imprisoned for treason. From his cell he wrote his manifesto *Mein Kampf* (*My Struggle*) in which he blamed Germany's decline on communists and Jews. Nobody could have realized his angry scribblings would be the blueprint for a horror to rival the First World War.

For much of the 1920s, the Nazis and communists vied with one another to topple the Weimar Republic but there was little public appetite for a revolution. However, in October 1929 the US Stock Market crashed resulting in an economic depression that was felt throughout the world. With six million unemployed, the Weimar Republic's social democracy looked utterly ineffective and the revolutionaries raced to fill the ideological void.

It was in this environment that Hitler led the Nazis to power in 1933. After the death of Germany's president, he dissolved the republic and declared himself absolute dictator (*Führer*) of the Third Reich ('Third Empire'). All rival political movements were subsequently outlawed or destroyed.

Over the next few years, Hitler set about rebuilding Germany's economy while brazenly violating the Treaty of Versailles. He rebuilt the German army and created the Luftwaffe - a powerful air force. He correctly anticipated that former Allied nations, who had no desire for another war, would not stop him. Bolstered by their timidity and his popularity at home, he turned his attention to reacquiring German territory.

In 1935, Saarland voted to leave France and return to German rule. A year later, German troops entered the Rhineland; this region was already administered by Germany but it had previously been an officially demilitarised area, and the Treaty of Versailles stated it must not host military forces or fortifications. The League of Nations offered no objections, and its member states attended the 1936 Berlin Olympics seemingly oblivious to the threat Hitler represented.

PUZZLE 69

What is missing from the Morse sequence below?

CLUE (Atbash): UREV GL MRMV NB WVZI DZGHLM

A STEP TOO FAR

The 1930s saw other nations forcefully expand their territories, testing the resolve of the League of Nations, which simply looked on disapprovingly. With the Great Depression keeping other nations quiet, Hitler believed the time was ripe to bring his plans to fruition.

In 1938 the Austrian government proposed a referendum on reunification with Germany. Uncertain of the outcome, Hitler decided to invade the country. His troops were greeted with widespread enthusiasm, and the annexation of Austria was accomplished without a shot fired.

Hitler's next target was the Sudetenland, an area in the north of Czechoslovakia with a large population of ethnic Germans. The Czechoslovakian military was in good shape and in no mood to be bullied, so an armed invasion seemed inevitable. The British, however, were desperate to maintain peace. Neville Chamberlain obtained a written promise from Hitler that he would end his expansionist plans if Britain recognized his claim to the Sudetenland. Chamberlain, pleased with the deal, declared it 'peace for our time'.

But Hitler was far from finished. After putting the rest of Czechoslovakia under German 'protection', he claimed the Danzig region of Poland. France and Britain finally understood his ambition and made it clear that entering Poland would be too much. Hitler dismissed this; having recently secured a non-aggression pact with the Soviet Union, he believed he had little to fear.

On 1 September 1939, Germany invaded Poland, joined by their Soviet ally 16 days later. Surrounded and outnumbered, the defenders were overwhelmed in just over a month.

France and Great Britain declared war on Germany on 3 September. It was now too late to prevent the storm about to ravage the world.

SOLUTIONS PAGE 199

PUZZLE 70

Here are the nicknames of some well-known Second World War personalities. Who are they?

1. Il Duce ....
2. Ike ....
3. Uncle Joe ....
4. The Constable ....
5. Tin Legs ....
6. The Forces' Sweetheart ....
7. Stuffy ....
8. The Desert Fox ....

PUZZLE 71

This sudoku has been encrypted with the letters **ADEHILNRS**. Solve it to find the word revealed in the shaded boxes.

	L				H			
			E	R				
A				N		R		
		R			A		E	I
	A		D		I		L	
I	E		R			S		
		H		L				
				D	R			
			H				I	

PUZZLE 72

Each letter of the alphabet has been encrypted to a number (1 to 26). Crack the code to solve the puzzle and reveal the political ideology hidden within. To start you off, the codes for three letters have been given.

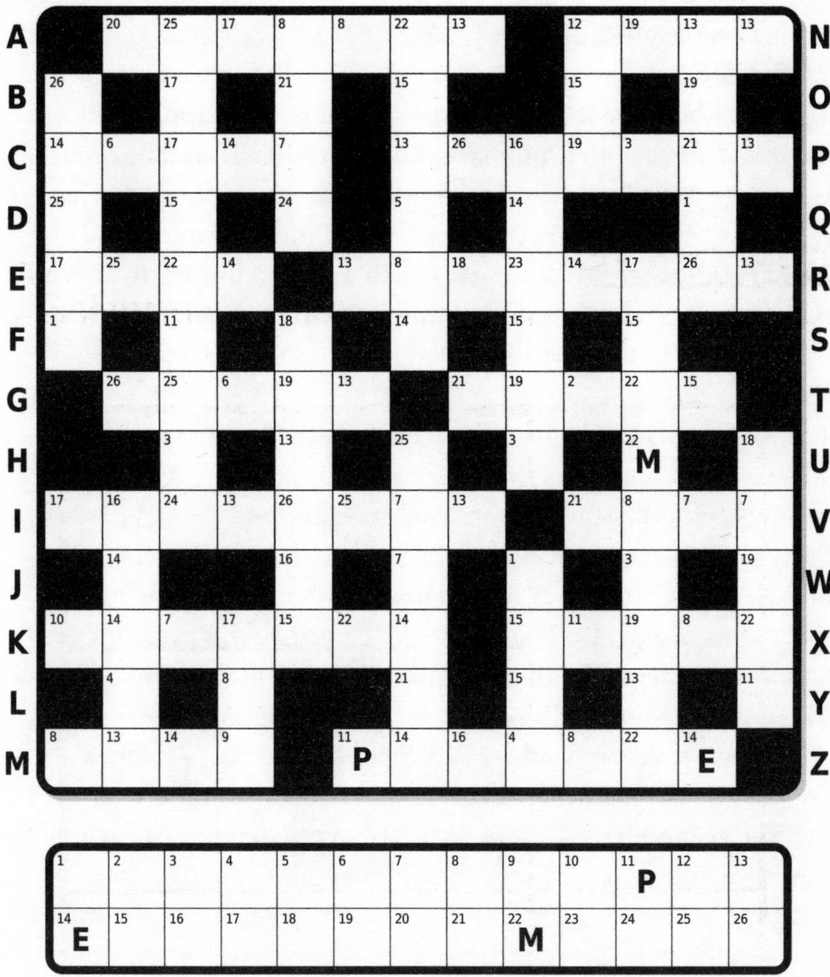

1	2	3	4	5	6	7	8	9	10	11	12	13
										P		
14	15	16	17	18	19	20	21	22	23	24	25	26
E								M				

SOLUTIONS PAGE 200-1

TAKING SIDES (PART II)

As with the First World War, the Second World War started as a conflict between two alliances but came to involve almost every nation around the world.

THE AXIS

To realize his expansionist dreams, Hitler had to supplement the use of force with diplomacy. The Third Reich and the Soviet Union were ideological enemies; their relationship was destined to be short-lived. However, Germany did form a more stable military alliance with other nations that shared its racially driven nationalism. These nations became collectively known as the Axis.

Italy

The Kingdom of Italy, like many other nations at the time, was going through a period of social and economic upheaval when Benito Mussolini assumed dictatorial control. His Fascist Party promised to restore the glory of the Roman Empire to the nation, and his policy of rapid militarization helped shield it from some of the effects of the Great Depression. Mussolini's apparent success during this period drew many admirers, among them Adolf Hitler. In 1934, Italy threatened the African nation of Abyssinia, whose leader Haile Selassie directly petitioned the League of Nations for help. The League's response was ineffective, and Italy's superior forces overwhelmed Abyssinia the following year. Mussolini then set about expanding his territory in North Africa and the Mediterranean, bringing Italy into conflict with Greece, Yugoslavia, France and Britain. He signed the Pact of Steel with Germany on 22 May 1939.

Japan

After fighting alongside the Allies in the First World War, Japan signed up to the League of Nations. Although purportedly a democracy, Japan still had imperial aspirations. Its rapidly growing economy lacked raw materials, so it looked towards the abundant resources in nearby Manchuria. In 1931, it launched a surprise attack and occupied the region. The League of Nations condemned the invasion but were powerless to intervene once Japan cancelled its membership. It then turned its attention to the rest of China, which was itself bogged down in a civil war between Communists and Nationalists. In 1936, before launching its next offensive, Japan signed a pact with Nazi Germany as a warning to their mutual rival, the Soviet Union. After a year of inflicting unprecedented barbarity on its neighbour, Japan came to occupy most of northern China, including the capital, Nanjing. It also attacked American merchant vessels travelling into China, and, on 12 December 1937, Japanese aircraft sank the US river gunboat USS *Panay*. Again the League of Nations did nothing. The United States, however, would not stand idly by for long.

Spain

In 1936, a brutal civil war broke out in Spain between the pro-monarchy Nationalists (an alliance of Falangists, Monarchists, Conservatives and Catholics) and pro-government/left-wing Republicans. Nationalist leader Francisco Franco turned to Hitler and Mussolini for help. Eager to test their newly modernized and expanded militaries, they agreed. Although volunteers from Britain and the United States came to help the Republicans, they were outmatched – Franco entered Madrid, proclaiming victory on 1 April 1939. Spain would remain neutral in the coming war, but the Nationalist victory convinced Hitler and Mussolini that they were unstoppable. As the leader of the Axis, Hitler was finally ready to put the plans he had outlined in *Mein Kampf* into motion.

THE ALLIES

Who would stand up to the rise of imperialist aggression? The League of Nations clearly had no stomach for conflict. And if its members could not protect one another collectively, what hope had individual nations against the power of the Axis?

Great Britain

Britain's post-First World War economy had not fully recovered and neither had its people. The government was resolved to keep the nation out of future wars and its scaled-down military could not be modernized during the economic hardship of the Great Depression. The Royal Navy, once the envy of the world, was now outnumbered in the Mediterranean by Mussolini's new fleet.

France

Like its Allied neighbour across the English Channel, France was still reeling from the First World War. It had suffered horrendous casualties, resulting in a manpower shortage for its largely conscript army. To compensate, it resorted to the First World War strategy of defence – a line of concrete fortifications on its borders with Germany, Italy, Switzerland and Luxembourg was constructed throughout the 1930s.

The Soviet Union

Following the Revolution of 1917, Russia and its satellites were transformed into a vast communist super-state. Its leader Joseph Stalin was concerned about Germany's rapid remilitarization and set about bolstering his own armed forces. To buy time, he signed a non-aggression pact with Germany mere days before their invasion of Poland, mainly because Stalin believed that the Western nations were failing to halt Hitler's territorial ambitions.

The United States

The United States had scaled down its military at the end of the Great War and was enjoying an economic and cultural boom during its period of isolation. But it was not to last. The Great Depression shook the nation, making it even less inclined to get involved in Europe's power struggles. Despite its professed disdain for empires, the US had overseas colonies of its own in the Pacific, which were under threat from Japanese expansionism. This rivalry would ultimately pull the US into the war.

China

China was one of the first countries to suffer from Axis aggression, but it had other problems. In 1912, the Qing Dynasty had been overthrown, ending 2,000 years of imperial rule. The republic that replaced it suffered a slew of internal conflicts, which led to a full-scale civil war between Communists and Nationalists in 1927. Japan was able to exploit this crisis and invaded the same year. Throughout the war, both Chinese factions received aid from the Soviet Union and United States to combat their mutual enemy, but it was not until 1941 that China formally joined the Allies.

PUZZLE 73

VIPS are often given code names to protect their identities. Can you identify the people in the photographs and put them together with their roles to determine their code name?

1. LIAM **2.** NANI **3.** BORE

4. THAG **5.** GENI **6.** DERN

CLUE (Atbash): ZMZTIZNH

Italian Prime Minister **AA** ....

British Prime Minister **AB** ....

American President **AC** ....

Soviet General Secretary **AD** ....

French Resistance Leader **EF** ....

Luftwaffe Supreme Commander **RG** ....

SOLUTIONS PAGE 201

THE INVASION OF POLAND

Poland's recent history had been one of subjugation. In the eighteenth century, Poland had been partitioned three times, with its territory reducing in size as Prussia, Russia and the Austrian Empire progressively absorbed more and more until, eventually, Poland was no longer a sovereign state. Despite becoming an independent nation after the First World War, its situation was still precarious, however, so it wisely sought an alliance with Britain and France.

Britain's recent treaty with Poland gave Hitler pause for thought. Before invading, he needed to justify his actions. Operation 'Himmler' was the Nazi plan to create the appearance of Polish aggression. In August 1939, fake attacks on German outposts were carried out by political soldiers (the SS and the SD) dressed in Polish uniforms. To add credibility to these incidents, several prisoners, dressed up as Polish soldiers, were murdered and left at the scene of the 'invasion'. Hitler was thus able to convince the German parliament that defensive action was required, both to protect German territory and the ethnic Germans in Poland.
On 1 September 1939, the newly modernized German Wehrmacht (the 'armed forces') invaded Poland.

PUZZLE 74

Operation 'Himmler' was known by another name. Can you find it by decrypting this ciphertext?

ABQDMFUAZ WAZEQDHQ

BLITZKRIEG

Poland never stood a chance. Its military was not only technologically inferior but also outnumbered. To make matters worse, while the Germans were mobilizing to the west, the Soviets were preparing an invasion in the east.

The Germans also unleashed a new type of warfare: Blitzkrieg (lightning war). The Blitzkrieg method of warfare was based on speed and mobility, bypassing static defences to strike deep into enemy territory in order to cut off supply and communication lines.

At the heart of Blitzkrieg was Germany's 2,500 Panzers (six armoured divisions and four light reconnaissance divisions), which outnumbered Poland's outdated tanks by at least three to one. The Panzers were supported by the vast German infantry as well as 1,300 aircraft. Poland had only 600 older (and in some cases obsolete) aircraft and unsurprisingly were not able to defend with them for long.

With its military obliterated, Warsaw surrendered on 27 September 1939. Despite the surrender, from September until the following January, occupying SS Einsatzgruppen carried out a programme of mass executions, murdering between 20,000 and 66,000 Poles, including hospital patients. The Soviet NKVD (secret police) behaved with similar barbarity, executing some 22,000 military officers and civilians who were deemed a threat. The two occupying powers then set about carving up the country.

The world was starting to learn the cost of appeasing the Führer.

SOLUTIONS PAGE 201

THE PHONEY WAR

France and Britain declared war on Germany on 3 September 1939, but little happened for the next eight months – a period that became known as the Phoney War.

Both countries mobilized their militaries and preparations were made for enemy air raids, including the evacuation of children from metropolitan areas. The British started sending troops to France, while France attempted an aborted invasion of Germany.

Britain initiated a naval blockade of German ports. This proved less effective than during the First World War because the Axis could obtain essential supplies via Spain and the Soviet Union. As before, Germany responded with submarine raids, which had a devastating effect on Allied merchant shipping due to insufficient Royal Navy escort vessels.

One event that might have changed history occurred on 8 November 1939: a bomb intended for Hitler killed eight people at a Munich beer hall. The Nazi leader had left the beer hall earlier than scheduled, just 13 minutes before the bomb exploded.

On 30 November 1939, the Soviet Union invaded Finland, which had become independent from Russia in 1918. With their enormous numerical advantage, the Soviets expected to win the Winter War easily, but the Finnish army, and the Finnish weather, had other ideas. Although Finland was eventually forced to cede territory to the invaders, it inflicted massive losses upon the Red Army. The Soviet Union was kicked out of the League of Nations and had been made to look weak. This was not lost on Hitler, who was waiting for the right moment to turn on his communist 'partners'.

The Allied nations also turned their attention towards Scandinavia – the Norwegian port of Narvik represented both a strategic and economic asset, as Germany depended on it to obtain iron ore from Sweden. However, diplomacy and dithering prevented the Allies from taking decisive action, and Germany began its invasion of Denmark and Norway on 9 April 1940. Denmark surrendered after a battle lasting less than two hours; Norway did the same after 62 days.

The Phoney War ended on 10 May 1940, which saw the Wehrmacht invade Belgium and Holland and Great Britain appoint a new prime minister: Winston Churchill.

FIRST WORLD WAR TANKS

Tanks were first seen on the battlefields of the First World War, and their technology developed fast. Britain developed ten different versions of tanks from Mark I to Mark X over the course of just three years, although some Marks such as VI and X were never produced.

Shown are four types – some looking rather the worse for wear after battle – **the Mark I, Mark II, Mark IV and Mark VIII. Can you identify them all successfully?**

1

2

SOLUTIONS PAGE 16

3

4

5

6

7
74

8
8

FIRST WORLD WAR GENERALS

Can you name these four generals, find the link that ties each of them to these battles or campaigns, and identify who is the odd one out?

Tannenberg, 1914

Gallipoli, 1915–16

Nivelle Offensive, 1917

Amiens, 1918

SOLUTIONS PAGE 16

SECOND WORLD WAR IN FIRST WORLD WAR

Each of the four men pictured below during the First World War went on to become Allied military leaders in the Second World War. Are you able to identify all four?
Note: the answer to picture 1 is the officer standing in the foreground, not the politician seated behind him. The answer to picture 4 is the Lieutenant Colonel showing the Montenegrin monarch an aerial camera.

One of these men had a very different experience to the other three in the First World War. Which was it, and why?
Hint: it had nothing to do with aeroplanes.

SOLUTIONS PAGE 16

THE WAR AT SEA

The four British ships shown are linked, and they can also be ordered in a particular way. Can you match the ship to the name, figure out what links them and put them in the correct order?

HMS Invincible

RMS Lusitania

HMS Indefatigable

HMS Queen Mary

SOLUTIONS PAGE 16

INTER-WAR CONFLICTS

Four conflicts are shown below. Each occurred during the 1930s, but before the outbreak of the Second World War. Can you identify each one, put them in date order and identify which is the odd one out?

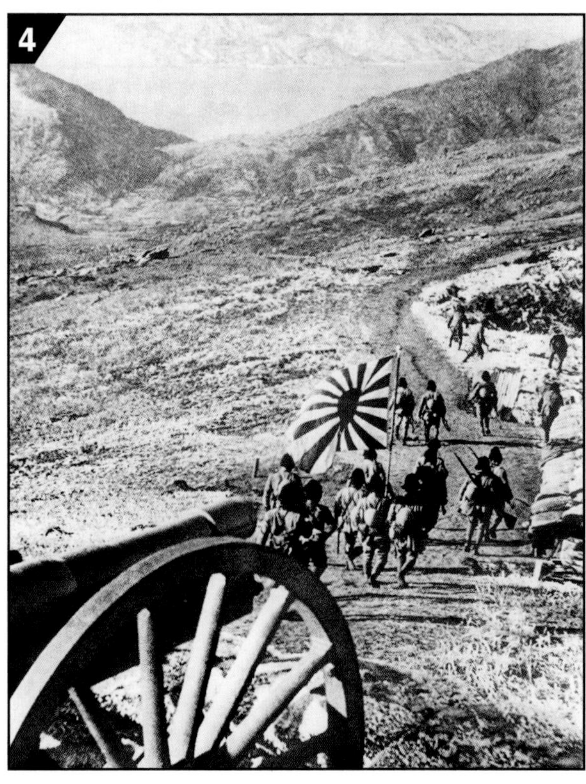

SOLUTIONS PAGE 16

THE BATTLE FOR THE SKIES

Combat in the air was of the utmost importance in the Second World War, and the Battle of Britain in particular has provided stories of legendary heroism and skill that still resonate today. Below are five iconic planes alongside a jumbled list of their nicknames. Can you match each image to its nickname and supply its proper name as well?

Nicknames: Flying Can Opener, Flying Fortress, Flying Pencil, Stuka, Whispering Death

SOLUTIONS PAGE 16

BRITISH LEADERS IN THE SECOND WORLD WAR

Below are six British military leaders alongside six listed theatres of war or operations. Can you identify each and match them to the conflict in which they played the largest part?

Battles/Operations:
Battle of the Atlantic, Battle of Britain, Battle of Dunkirk, Battle of the Mediterranean, Battle of the Ruhr, Operation Market Garden

SOLUTIONS PAGE 16

SOLUTIONS

FIRST WORLD WAR TANKS

1. British Mark II tank
2. British Mark IV tank
3. British Mark IV tank
4. British Mark I tank
5. British Mark VIII tank
6. British Mark VIII tank
7. British Mark II tank
8. British Mark I tank

FIRST WORLD WAR GENERALS

1. Russian General Alexander Samsonov
2. British General Ian Hamilton
3. French General Robert Nivelle
4. German General Georg von der Marwitz

Each general was in command of what is generally accepted to be the losing side of the named battles. The odd one out is General Samsonov, who committed suicide while retreating from the battlefield after the Russian Second Army was almost completely destroyed under his command. The other generals all continued their service, although Nivelle was demoted and Hamilton was recalled and given no further commands.

SECOND WORLD WAR IN FIRST WORLD WAR

1. Field Marshal Bernard Montgomery
2. General Dwight D. Eisenhower
3. General Douglas MacArthur
4. Air Chief Marshal Hugh Dowding

Eisenhower's First World War experience was markedly different from the others as, despite numerous requests to serve overseas, he remained in the USA throughout, serving at various training camps.

Meanwhile, MacArthur received, among other awards, seven Silver Stars for his war efforts. Dowding flew during the war and was appointed a Companion of the Order of St Michael and St George. Montgomery was wounded… twice.

THE ROYAL NAVY

1. HMS *Indefatigable*
2. RMS *Lusitania*
3. HMS *Queen Mary*
4. HMS *Invincible*

All four of these ships was unfortunately sunk during the First World War. Even worse, their sinkings were the four most deadly of British ships. The correct order is:
1,266 people – HMS *Queen Mary*
1,198 people – RMS *Lusitania*
1,026 people – HMS *Invincible*
1,015 people – HMS *Indefatigable*

INTER-WAR CONFLICTS

4. The Japanese invasion of China/ Manchuria (1931)
2. The Italian invasion of Ethiopia/ Abyssinia (1935)
3. The Spanish Civil War (1936)
1. The German invasion of Poland (1939)

The odd one out is the Spanish Civil War. All of the other conflicts were invasions and, although there were many international soldiers who fought in the Spanish Civil War, it was essentially an internal conflict.

THE BATTLE FOR THE SKIES

1. Stuka – Junkers Ju 87.
2. Flying Fortress – Boeing B-17.
3. Flying Pencil – Dornier Do 17.
4. Whispering Death – Bristol Beaufighter, specifically Type 156.
5. Flying Can Opener – Hawker Hurricane, specifically the Mark IID flown by the No.6 Squadron of the RAF.

BRITISH LEADERS IN THE SECOND WORLD WAR

1. Admiral of the Fleet Alfred Pound – Battle of the Atlantic
2. Field Marshal Bernard Montgomery – Operation Market Garden
3. Air Chief Marshal Arthur Harris – Battle of the Ruhr
4. Field Marshal Harold Alexander – Battle of Dunkirk
5. Air Chief Marshal Hugh Dowding – Battle of Britain
6. Admiral of the Fleet Andrew Cunningham – Battle of the Mediterranean

PUZZLE 75

Test your general knowledge of the Second World War. What was…

1. A doodlebug?
2. *Anschluss*?
3. Hobart's Funnies?
4. The *Maquis*?
5. *Sitzkrieg*?

PUZZLE 76

Battleships! Find the enemy fleet on the grid below. The numbers on the periphery tell you how many occupied squares are in that row or column. No two vessels occupy neighbouring squares (including diagonals). There are four kinds of vessel and the number of each type in the fleet is as follows:

Battleship	◀■■▶ x1	**Destroyer**	◀▶ x3
Cruiser	◀■▶ x2	**Submarine**	■ x4

	3	1	3	1	3	1	3	1	2	2	
3									◀		3
5											5
0											0
1											1
3					■						3
1											1
2											2
3							■				3
0											0
2									◀		2
	3	1	3	1	3	1	3	1	2	2	

SOLUTIONS PAGE 202

THE FALL OF FRANCE

Hitler was exuberant after his successful campaigns in Poland and Scandinavia. The Allied response had been slow and ineffective, and he was eager to press his advantage. However, the Poles had not gone down without a fight, and he was forced to wait while his forces recovered and regrouped.

Believing the next conflict would be a repeat of the First World War, France had invested heavily in fortified defences. The Maginot Line was constructed along the border with Germany, from Switzerland all the way up to Belgium, and was believed to be impregnable.

There was concern that Hitler would employ the same opening gambit that the German Empire had used at the start of the First World War. The Schlieffen Plan had involved sending the bulk of Germany's forces through Belgium to outflank France's army and take Paris. The plan had failed in 1914 and both sides had become bogged down in trench warfare.

Germany's situation was different in 1940: it was not waging a simultaneous war against Russia; and it had its new Blitzkrieg tactic. With French and British troops assembling on the Belgian border, the Germans decided to deploy its forces further south, at the point where the Maginot Line ended: the Ardennes.

The Allies' ground forces had a numerical advantage and were at least equal to the Wehrmacht in terms of technology, training and fitness. But they were distributed thinly along the Maginot Line and the Belgian border. The Luftwaffe also had a far greater number of fighters and bombers. Furthermore, the Allies had overlooked the defence of the Ardennes because it was judged unsuitable terrain for a tank assault. This judgement proved to be fatally flawed.

German Field Marshal Gerd von Rundstedt directed his main assault force through the Ardennes, and the lead elements of Heinz Guderian's XIX Panzer Corps encountered French forces on 11 May 1940. The rest of the Corps roared out of the forest and, after crossing the River Meuse, the Germans engaged French forces at Sedan and were ultimately victorious. Guderian, a master of Blitzkrieg, pushed on with his Panzers, leaving the slower troops behind. By 20 May, he had taken the towns of Amiens and Abbeville and reached the coast.

In the north, Belgium and Holland had been completely overrun. Once again, the German surge had proved irrepressible. After just two and a half weeks of fighting, the outflanked French, Belgian and British forces were pushed back to the sea. Cut off in the coastal cities of Calais, Boulogne and Dunkirk, they awaited their fate.

PUZZLE 77

Can you unscramble the surnames of six Second World War leaders below, which have each had their letters jumbled up and some spaces introduced? One extra letter has been added to each name which, when all six are extracted and read in order from top to bottom, will spell out a word which connects the names.

AUNT MAR ....

CHILL LURCH ....

SOLE REVOLT ....

SIN TAIL ....

ABLER MACHINE ....

DUAL LEDGE ....

SOLUTIONS PAGE 202

DUNKIRK

Calais and Boulogne eventually fell to German assaults, but on 23 May Field Marshal von Rundstedt halted the advance intended to finish off the Allies in Dunkirk. The rapid deployment of the Panzers had stretched German lines to near breaking point and they now needed to recover. The brief reprieve gave the defenders just enough time to fortify their positions and plan an evacuation.

When the advance recommenced on 27 May, another opportunity came the Allies' way. Torrential rain had turned the ground to mud, and the Blitzkrieg was forced to squelch forward at a reduced pace. That same day, Vice Admiral Bertram Ramsay of the Royal Navy received the order to commence Operation 'Dynamo' – the evacuation of troops from Dunkirk.

The port had been bombed, making it difficult to get the men to larger naval vessels – although fortunately the eastern mole was still intact, from which most of the men were later to be evacuated on to Royal Navy vessels. Nevertheless, a call went out for any smaller craft to help. Over 800 fishing boats, lifeboats, barges, yachts and other small vessels from the south coast of England answered the call. These were able to ferry some of the troops from the coast of Dunkirk to the larger Royal Navy ships out at sea. They did so under constant bombardment from the Luftwaffe and, although the Royal Air Force launched a desperate defence, an estimated 18 warships and almost a quarter of the civilian vessels were sunk.

On 4 June, the evacuation was halted. British armour and artillery had to be abandoned but more than 300,000 troops had been rescued thanks to the 'Little Ships of Dunkirk', the bravery of the crews of the Royal Navy vessels and the heroism of the French rearguard, who held off the German advance while their comrades were evacuated.

France was now effectively defenceless, its Maginot Line useless and, with over half its army lost, could do nothing to turn the tide of Panzers and Luftwaffe bombers. On 14 June, the German army marched into Paris. With the majority of French ministers favouring peace talks, Prime Minister Paul Reynaud resigned on 16 June and was replaced by Marshal Philippe Pétain, who signed an armistice with Germany on 22 June.

PUZZLE 78

In a motorcade consisting of motorbikes (no sidecars) and cars (four wheels), there are 72 vehicles and 200 wheels. How many motorbikes are there?

PUZZLE 79

Place 0, 1 or 2 mines into some of the empty cells so that each number represents the total count of mines in neighbouring cells, including diagonally adjacent cells.

2	2	2		1		
			2		3	2
2		3		4		
	2			4		2
2		5		2	3	3
4			6			
	6		5		3	2

SOLUTIONS PAGE 203

OCCUPATION AND RESISTANCE

Marshal Pétain was a hero of the First World War but under his administration France became an authoritarian regime. Germany did not simply annex France but split it into two zones: a military occupied zone in the north, and a 'free' zone in the south. The administrative capital was moved from Paris to Vichy in the 'free' zone.

One of the terms of the armistice was that the French Navy should remain in its ports. The British demanded that French ships docked in North Africa be handed over to the Allies but Pétain declined, so the British attacked and crippled the fleet, killing over 1,000 French naval personnel in the process. This ruthless act might have been strategically critical, but it soured relationships with a France that already felt abandoned by its former ally.

Many French collaborated with the German occupiers: some sympathized with Germany's aims; some were anti-communists; and others complied under sufferance. But there were also a few men and women prepared to risk their lives rather than accept Nazi rule. The Resistance was not a single entity, but rather a scattering of groups with different politics, ranging from conservative Catholics to communists. An attempt to unify them was made by Charles de Gaulle, the former undersecretary for war, who had refused to sign the armistice and escaped to England. He was initially marginalized by the Allies since both the United States and the Soviet Union recognized Pétain's 'Vichy France'. However, his stubborn determination to rally the French would gain more traction as the extent of the Nazis' atrocities came to light.

PUZZLE 80

For each of the words below add or remove one letter – without changing the original order – to create a new word. Make a note of the 12 letters that you added or removed to find the name of a Second World War personality.

ARGON		NEW	
SOON		TRUST	
TEAM		RID	
EMOTION		LAIR	
STRIPPED		COINED	
LATER		LACE	

PUZZLE 81

Can you find five vehicle- and vehicle detection-themed words related to the Second World War hidden in the sentences below? For example, the word 'plane' is hidden in the sentence 'We should <u>plan e</u>verything thoroughly'.

1. The troops in Stalingrad are determined not to surrender.
2. The army had victory in its grasp; it fired relentlessly at the enemy lines.
3. Japan zeroed in on Pearl Harbor as a target later in the war.
4. Success depends on a replenished air force.
5. The intelligence officer still needs her mandatory field training.

SOLUTIONS PAGE 203-4

BRITAIN AT WAR

With the capitulation of France on 22 June 1940, Britain stood alone. Its vast Empire had mobilized but was too thinly stretched where it was needed. Hitler considered it just a matter of time before the British sought an armistice; his previous meeting with former Prime Minister Neville Chamberlain would certainly have reinforced this conviction.

But the new prime minister was different. Although acutely aware of Britain's precarious situation, Winston Churchill refused to yield to Nazi aggression, even when Hitler offered peace in exchange for non-intervention. Churchill's rousing speeches instilled pride and defiance into a nation still reeling from the retreat at Dunkirk. Britain would fight on.

But for all his fiery rhetoric, Churchill was in no position to launch a counteroffensive. Britain's armour and artillery had been left on the beaches of northern France and its 25 divisions of rifle-armed infantry would be impotent against the hordes of German Panzers.

Britain had no option but to dig in. Its key defensive advantage lay in being an island. If Hitler wanted to invade the country, he would have to contend with the Royal Navy Home Fleet and newly constructed coastal defences. Realizing this, Hitler turned his attention to the skies.

PUZZLE 82

Here are extracts from some of Winston Churchill's most famous speeches. Can you decrypt them and put them in chronological order?

1 NVM DROO HGROO HZB GSRH DZH GSVRI URMVHG SLFI

2 DV HSZOO URTSG RM GSV SROOH DV HSZOO MVEVI HFIIVMWVI

3 MVEVI RM GSV URVOW LU SFNZM XLMUORXG DZH HL NFXS LDVW YB HL NZMB GL HL UVD

4 R SZEV MLGSRMT GL LUUVI YFG YOLLW, GLRO, GVZIH ZMW HDVZG

The Nazi plan to invade Britain was code-named 'Seelöwe' ('Sea Lion'). Hitler surmised that if he achieved absolute air superiority, he could bomb the Home Fleet to extinction and pave the way for an amphibious assault. He hoped that removing the RAF would be a mere formality – the reality, however, was to prove to be quite different.

PUZZLE 83

Each letter of the alphabet has been encrypted to a number (1 to 26). Crack the code to solve the puzzle and reveal the diplomatic policy hidden within. To start you off, the codes for three letters have been given.

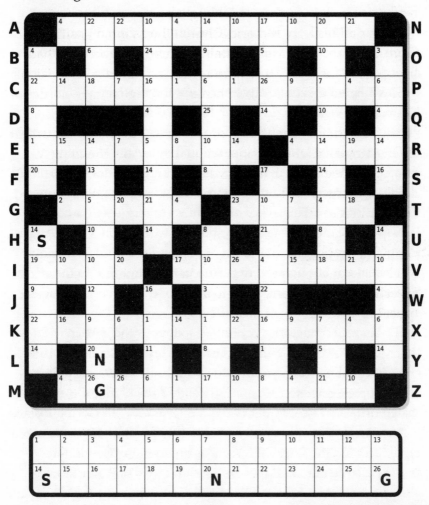

A		4	22	22	10	4	14	10	17	10	20	21		N
B	4		6		24		9		5		10		3	O
C	22	14	18	7	16	1	6	1	26	9	7	4	6	P
D	8				4		25		14		10		4	Q
E	1	15	14	7	5	8	10	14		4	14	19	14	R
F	20		13		14		8		17		14		16	S
G		2	5	20	21	4		23	10	7	4	18		T
H	14 S		10		14		8		21		8		14	U
I	19	10	10	20		17	10	26	4	15	18	21	10	V
J	9		12		16		3		22				4	W
K	22	16	9	6	1	14	1	22	16	9	7	4	6	X
L	14		20 N		11		8		1		5		14	Y
M		4	26 G	26	6	1	17	10	8	4	21	10		Z

1	2	3	4	5	6	7	8	9	10	11	12	13
14	**15**	**16**	**17**	**18**	**19**	**20**	**21**	**22**	**23**	**24**	**25**	**26**
S						N						G

SOLUTIONS PAGE 204-5

THE BATTLE OF BRITAIN

On 10 July 1940, the Luftwaffe began bombing British ships in the English Channel in preparation for Operation 'Sea Lion'. The battle for Britain would now be decided in the air.

The responsibility for coordinating RAF Fighter Command fell to Air Chief Marshal Hugh Dowding. His immediate problem was that he had roughly the same number of single-seat fighters as the Luftwaffe – 754 to the Germans' 805. However, he did not know where they might appear; clearly the RAF could not simply patrol and hope to successfully engage with every air attack. Dowding, therefore, invested in a recent technological innovation: radio detection and ranging (RADAR). A chain of radar masts along the south and east coast warned of imminent German raids while the Royal Observer Corps identified the number of enemy aircraft involved. This allowed him to pick his engagements and focus on air superiority rather than respond to every bombing raid.

Dowding's immediate adversary was the Reichsmarschall Hermann Göring. Still flush with his successes in Poland and France, Göring was confident he could defeat the RAF within days. On 13 August, he launched Operation 'Eagle Attack' aiming to completely destroy RAF fighters, airfields and production facilities.

The day before, the Luftwaffe had raided radar stations and the buildings at Ventnor, Isle of Wight were seriously damaged. However, the radar system was still able to function. On 13 August, most of the airfields in the south of England endured a ferocious bombardment but none were permanently damaged. In the air, the balance of victories went to the RAF, who lost between 13 and 15 aircraft compared to the Luftwaffe's 44.

The balance of victories continued to favour the RAF in the days that followed – but it could not last. With fewer aircraft and trained crew, RAF pilots were required to fly multiple sorties each day and became exhausted. Operation 'Eagle Attack' might well have sealed Britain's fate if Hitler had not interfered with Göring's plans.

After an RAF bomber raid on the night of 25 August, an enraged Hitler ordered the Luftwaffe to focus on bombing London instead. In a speech, he raged, 'If they declare that they will attack our cities on a large scale, we will erase theirs!' This gave the RAF vital respite and a renewed determination. Their resolve, combined with the radar-enhanced ability to hunt down enemy aircraft, started to wear down the Luftwaffe's morale. As the days rolled on and their planes continued to fall from the sky, it became clear that Operation 'Sea Lion' was untenable. On 31 October 1940, the Battle of Britain came to an end. Unfortunately, the bombing did not.

The Aeroplanes

Military aircraft had advanced considerably since the First World War. Here are just some of the aircraft that dominated the skies during the Battle of Britain.

LUFTWAFFE

Junkers Ju 88

The most modern and effective of Germany's fast bombers, the twin-engine Ju 88 had a maximum airspeed of 290 mph and could carry around 4,000 lbs of bombs.

Messerschmitt Bf 109

The core of the Luftwaffe's fighter force, the Bf 109 was one of the most advanced fighters in the world with a top speed of 350 mph. They were used primarily to escort the German bombers.

Junkers Ju 87

This *Sturzkampfflugzeug* (dive bomber) became infamously known by its abbreviation: Stuka. Capable of precision ground strikes from a near-vertical dive, the Ju 87 was a terrifying and effective part of the invasion of Poland, especially those Stukas fitted with 'Jericho trumpet' sirens, which provoked both shock and awe in their targets. The dive-bomber sound lives on in popular culture.

ROYAL AIR FORCE

Supermarine Spitfire

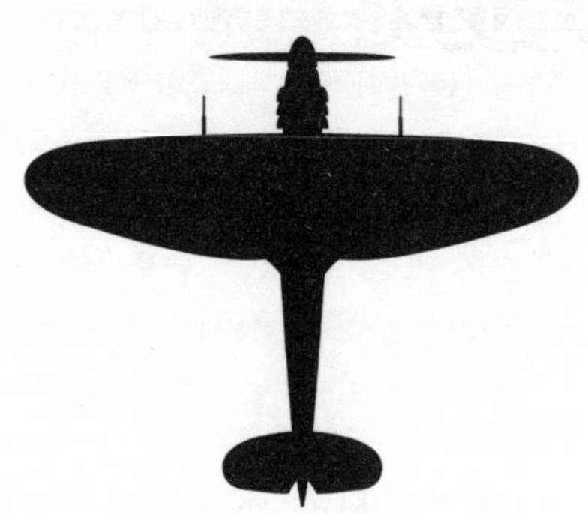

Slightly faster and more agile than the Bf 109, this state-of-the-art fighter had distinctive elliptical wings which were thin enough to avoid excessive drag but thick enough to accommodate the plane's firepower and retractable landing gear. It came to symbolize Britain's resistance throughout the war.

Hawker Hurricane

The bane of German bombers, the Hawker Hurricane was the most numerous RAF fighter. Tough and easy to maintain, it was considered the 'workhorse' to the Spitfire's 'thoroughbred'. Although it lacked the speed of the Bf 109, it could out-turn one in a dogfight. German pilots preferred to avoid prolonged contact with Hurricanes and would instead use 'dive and zoom' tactics from a higher altitude. It was the Hurricane, not the more celebrated Spitfire, that shot down the most enemy aircraft during the Battle of Britain.

PUZZLE 84

An exhausted RAF pilot has just returned from a day of dogfighting against the Luftwaffe. He is not required to be on duty until 10am the following morning but does not want to be late, so he sets his extremely loud alarm clock for 8.45am. After a mug of Ovaltine, the pilot falls asleep at 8.15pm. How long does he sleep for?

PUZZLE 85

You are in charge of RAF Fighter Command, and we have incoming enemy bombers! On the grid below, you must attach a Spitfire to each enemy bomber.

- Place each Spitfire in a square adjacent to its target, immediately to its north, south, east or west – not diagonal.

- No Spitfire can occupy a square that shares an edge or corner with another Spitfire's square.

- The numbers in the periphery tell you exactly how many Spitfires must be assigned to that row or column.

	2	1	0	2	0	2	2	1	
1									1
1									1
1									1
1									1
2									2
1									1
1									1
2									2
	2	1	0	2	0	2	2	1	

SOLUTIONS PAGE 205

BOMBED BUT NOT OUT

After abandoning his plans to invade Britain, Hitler ordered the strategic bombing campaign to continue and switched the Luftwaffe to night-time operations. Night after night the inhabitants of major cities were subjected to a relentless bombardment, which they called the Blitz.

The British population rallied to protect their nation. Men who were not eligible for full military service signed up with the Home Guard; the prospect of a German invasion remained a threat even though the Battle of Britain had put Hitler off the idea.

Children had already been evacuated from vulnerable towns and cities and taken to the countryside and blackouts were strictly enforced in Britain from 1 September 1939. Women once again found employment in armaments factories and in the Land Army, doing important agricultural work.

It was not until 10 May 1941 that London was forced to endure its last air raid, but both morale and military production had held strong throughout. Over 50,000 civilians lost their lives in the Blitz. The endurance of the British in the face of this horror earned sympathetic admiration abroad.

PUZZLE 86

Some nights there was little to do in the air-raid shelter except enquire into other people's business.

'How old are your three little 'uns?' asked nosey Nora.

'If you add their ages together, you get 13. If you multiply them, 36,' replied cryptic Cathy.

'Are two of them twins?'

'Yes.'

'What are their names?'

'Lucy and Helen.'

Nora's brow creased in thought.

'My eldest is a girl, too,' added Cathy.

'Aha!' exclaimed Nora triumphantly, for now she knew the children's ages.

How old are Cathy's children? And how did Nora work it out?

PUZZLE 87

In the word search below are the names of British cities that were targeted during the Blitz. They may appear horizontally, vertically or diagonally, backwards or forwards. Can you find them?

K	N	Y	H	T	U	O	M	S	T	R	O	P	C	R
L	C	O	P	I	L	Y	W	X	M	M	I	Q	M	B
I	W	W	G	L	Y	T	S	A	F	L	E	B	R	U
V	L	B	U	A	E	S	N	A	W	S	Q	I	Q	D
E	V	H	B	Y	Q	C	U	Y	Z	X	S	B	N	L
R	Y	S	E	I	H	G	C	Q	F	T	P	O	S	E
P	F	A	V	E	L	R	P	J	O	L	T	T	X	I
O	P	G	S	A	M	F	L	L	Y	P	J	Y	O	F
O	E	T	S	C	F	L	U	M	M	Q	Q	R	C	F
L	E	G	L	I	H	P	O	A	H	B	B	T	A	E
R	O	V	D	W	D	U	H	N	A	U	O	N	L	H
W	Y	R	M	G	T	T	K	L	D	R	P	E	Z	S
H	A	H	N	H	U	H	Z	X	G	O	H	V	L	B
C	S	K	U	O	G	A	O	I	T	S	N	O	H	L
A	S	L	S	G	P	I	Y	K	V	I	I	C	I	S

The list of cities has been encrypted using the Atbash cipher.

YVOUZHG
YIRHGLO
XZIWRUU
XLEVMGIB
TOZHTLD
SFOO
OREVIKLLO
OLMWLM
NZMXSVHGVI
KOBNLFGS
KLIGHNLFGS
HSVUURVOW
HLFGSZNKGLM
HDZMHVZ

SOLUTIONS PAGE 206

PUZZLE 88

Three SOE agents have been dispatched to different locations in occupied France. Each agent is given a code name and assigned to a network. From the three clues below, can you work out each agent's assignment?

1. Nora was attached to the 'Cinema' network; her code name was not *Lise*.
2. Yvonne's code name was *Annette*, she was not sent to Paris and her network was not 'Spindle'.
3. *Lise* was sent to Annecy in the French Alps.

	Annette	Madeleine	Lise	Paris	Annecy	Bordeaux	Spindle	Wheelwright	Cinema
Odette									
Nora									
Yvonne									
Spindle									
Wheelwright									
Cinema									
Paris									
Annecy									
Bordeaux									

Agent	Code Name	Location	Network

FIGHTING DIRTY, FIGHTING BACK

Britain had shown that it could take a beating. But Dunkirk had been a retreat and the Battle of Britain little more than a respite. Churchill wanted to take the war to the Nazis but he had no allies and was outmatched in terms of manpower and firepower. Britain would need to employ stealth and guile.

MI6

The Secret Service Bureau, founded in 1909, had a foreign intelligence division that had enjoyed only limited success during the First World War. After the war, this division was named the Secret Intelligence Service (SIS) and improved its network by working within the diplomatic service and the passport office.

The SIS was so secret that even members of the government were unaware of its existence – a counterproductive state of affairs, especially when it required resources. In 1939, Stewart Menzies, a counter-intelligence specialist during the First World War, became Chief of the SIS. He set about expanding its remit and getting the funds it needed to become an effective weapon against the Nazis.

The United States was impressed by the organization of the British SIS – despite its shoestring budget – and used it as a template for its own Office of Strategic Services (OSS). The countries shared techniques and intelligence even while the US was neutral in the war.

The ability to keep secret information secret is of paramount importance in wartime. Conversely, wars can be won by breaking enemy codes. The subdivision of the SIS charged with decrypting enemy communications was the Government Code and Cypher School (GC&CS), which had been part of the Admiralty during the First World War but transferred to the Foreign Office in 1922.

Based at an old mansion in Bletchley Park, the GC&CS codebreakers were a colourful assortment of men and women, scholars, linguists and mathematicians, all with a highly analytical, puzzle-solving mindset.

SOLUTIONS PAGE 206

ENIGMA VS ULTRA

The Wehrmacht used an encryption system known as Enigma. Although essentially a polyalphabetic substitution cipher, Enigma was substantially more sophisticated than the pen and paper techniques described earlier in this book, because it was encrypted with an electronic machine.

German engineer Arthur Scherbius had invented the Enigma machine in the 1920s to keep commercial messages secret. With the outbreak of war, the Heer (army), Kriegsmarine (navy) and Luftwaffe all developed their own versions.

The Enigma machine looked like an unusual typewriter. When a plaintext letter was typed on its keyboard, an electric current passed through a rotor mechanism to light up a ciphertext letter on its lamp board. This action would then advance one or more of the rotors, so that even if the same letter were pressed again, it would most likely yield a different result.

The ciphertext was transmitted in Morse code and decrypted by an Enigma operator at the receiving end, who would know the precise configuration of elements (rotors, rings and plugboard) which served as Enigma's key.

The three rotors were removable and interchangeable, and the operator had five to choose from. Each rotor had 26 settings, corresponding to the letters of the alphabet.

PUZZLE 89

What is the number of possible …

1. rotor combinations?
2. start settings for the three rotors?

The adjustable rings altered the rate at which the rotors advanced after each key press, while the plugboard provided an additional layer of encryption: a straight substitution cipher for ten pairs of letters.

A message typed on an Enigma machine could be encrypted in over 100 billion ways, creating a code the Germans understandably believed to be unbreakable. The Wehrmacht entrusted almost all of their war communications to Enigma, so cracking it was the top priority for the Bletchley Park team.

However, the first agency to make a dent in Enigma's armour was the Biuro Szyfrów (the Polish Cipher Bureau). They had the good fortune to come across a commercial version of the machine before the war and set their top mathematicians to cracking its code. They were assisted by French intelligence, who had infiltrated the Wehrmacht's Cipher Department and supplied essential information about the workings of the military version.

The Polish codebreakers were able to reconstruct their own Enigma machines and intercept some German communications, but the process was laborious and when the Wehrmacht made modifications to the system, their efforts suffered a setback. Less than a month before their country was overrun by the Nazis, they took their findings to Great Britain.

The information provided by Polish intelligence was invaluable. The Allied codebreakers now knew that their enemy was not human ingenuity but a machine that could process information faster than a whole legion of experts. The machine had been built by humans, so a team of equally clever humans could surely create a machine to beat it.

Among the exceptional men and women recruited to solve this puzzle were the mathematicians Alan Turing and Gordon Welchman, who made significant improvements to the Polish decryption devices known as bomba. With a combination of tenacity, desperation, genius and good fortune, their team made a device that would allow the Allies to intercept German military communications almost as fast as they were transmitted.

PUZZLE 90

Can you decrypt this message – which is part of a quote – and guess who it refers to?

HEAGEGHDLGEATDSTSLENETIOGETHEX

CLUE (Atbash): YIRGRHS HOZMT ULI Z TOZMXV

SOLUTIONS PAGE 206-7

PUZZLE 91

Today, the Secret Intelligence Service is more commonly known as MI6. Its first director was Captain Sir Mansfield Smith-Cumming, who unwittingly created the single-letter code name that has been given to all subsequent SIS chiefs. **What is the letter?**

Churchill recognized the vital contribution to the war effort made by the Bletchley Park codebreakers and referred to their achievements as his 'ultra-secret', which is how the division and its work became known by the code name 'Ultra'.

Cracking Enigma was not down to just one person, group or machine. The codebreakers at Bletchley Park were assigned a wide variety of tasks, one of the most important being the evaluation of enemy 'crib' (decrypted plaintext). Tried and tested methods from earlier centuries were employed to identify patterns in the behaviour of Enigma's human operators. A famous example was the habit of the Germans signing off their messages with 'Heil Hitler'.

Although the Germans were oblivious to the success of Ultra, they continued to refine their encryption. The Kriegsmarine added a fourth rotor to their Enigma machines, but Turing modified his bombes and the playing field was levelled once again.

While German tactical communications were entrusted to Enigma, from 1940 onwards a more sophisticated machine known as Lorenz performed high-level strategic encryption. This cryptographic device had twelve rotors and settings beyond the 26-letter alphabet. Hitler himself used the machine to send top-secret messages, but another brilliant British mathematician, William Tutte, broke the Lorenz code without even having access to the device.

Ultra provided the Allies with a wealth of information about enemy positions and forthcoming attacks, so it was essential the Germans did not become suspicious that their code had been cracked. This meant that not every piece of intelligence could be acted upon. The SIS even created a fictional super-spy called 'Boniface' which led the Germans to believe he or she was responsible for obtaining intelligence from an espionage network within the Third Reich.

PUZZLE 92

Each letter of the alphabet has been encrypted to a number (1 to 26). Crack the code to solve the puzzle and reveal the military tactic hidden within. To start you off, the codes for three letters have been given.

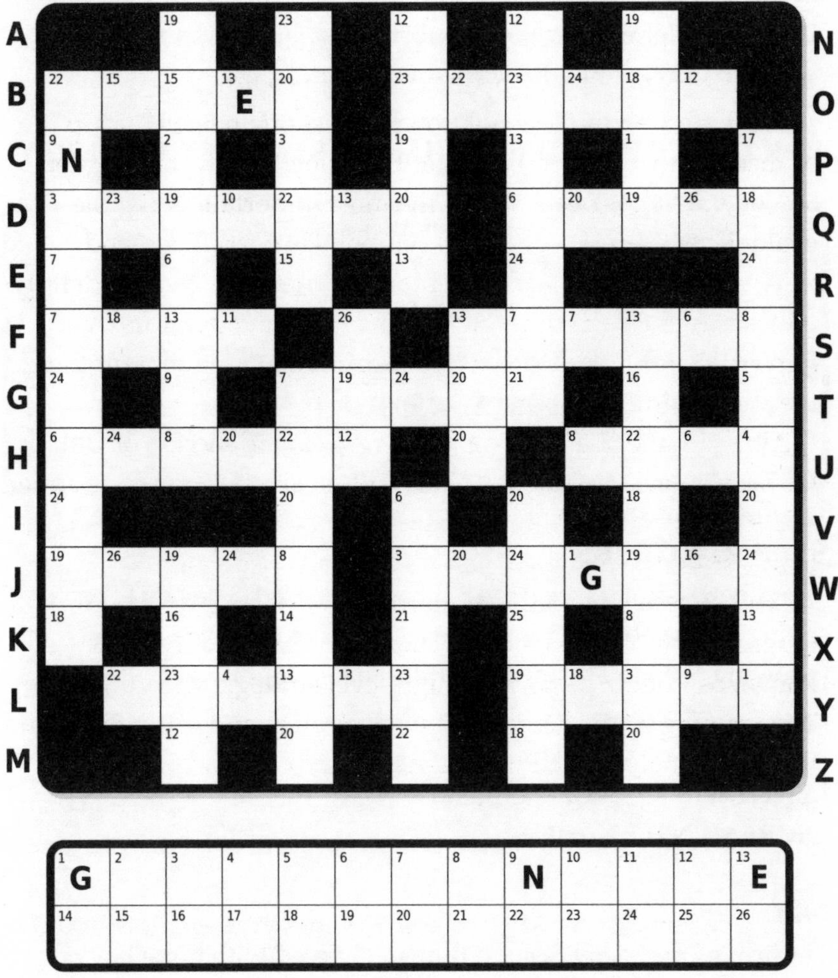

SOLUTIONS PAGE 208

PUZZLE 93

The following message has been double-encrypted. A Bletchley Park codebreaker could probably have solved it in their tea break. **Do you have what it takes?**

KQRGUZZJDQDVWZZWIFOXFYEAXUUCIM
UBLWOLTGNOFSMAAEABZDMMETCGU
CRQVXMTXKYYTEKWLYOXSOZM

STEP 1: PLUGBOARD

Ten pairs of letters have been substituted. Below is a famous pangram encrypted with the same cipher:

RPK QUYCE ZTSGD FSX JUAHKN SLKT RPK VMBI NSW

Plaintext												
a	b	c	d	e	f	g	h	i	j	k	l	m
		C			F				J			
Ciphertext												

Plaintext												
n	o	p	q	r	s	t	u	v	w	x	y	z
			Q				U			X		
Ciphertext												

STEP 2: ROTORS

The Alberti Cipher (see page 32) has been used. The key to each setting can be obtained from the last digit of the years in which the following Second World War battles were fought.

START: El Alamein
LENGTH: Monte Cassino
INCREMENT: Kursk

MI5

The arm of the Secret Service Bureau charged with homeland security and counter-intelligence was (and still is) MI5. At the start of the war, the department was a shambles – Churchill was forced to replace its director twice before it became an effective agency.

In the build-up to the aborted Operation 'Sea Lion', the Abwehr (German military intelligence) realized that their spy network in Britain was inadequate. As a result, they launched Operation 'Lena' in 1940, which sent some 20 spies across the Channel by boat or parachute.

'Lena', however, was a catastrophic failure for the Axis. Many of the spies spoke poor or heavily accented English and were unable to blend into a populace already on high alert for a Nazi invasion. They were quickly rounded up and sent to MI5 for interrogation.

MI5 ran a highly effective '*Double Cross*' (XX) project, which offered captured enemy agents the option of defecting as an alternative to imprisonment or execution. It was ultimately able to neutralize or turn all German spies that were sent to Britain during the war.

In the murky world of espionage, nothing is clear-cut. There have been suggestions that the Abwehr's incompetence was a deliberate act of sabotage by anti-Nazi elements in the German military. Admiral Wilhelm Canaris, the head of the Abwehr, was executed for treason in 1945.

PUZZLE 94

What makes this statement true?

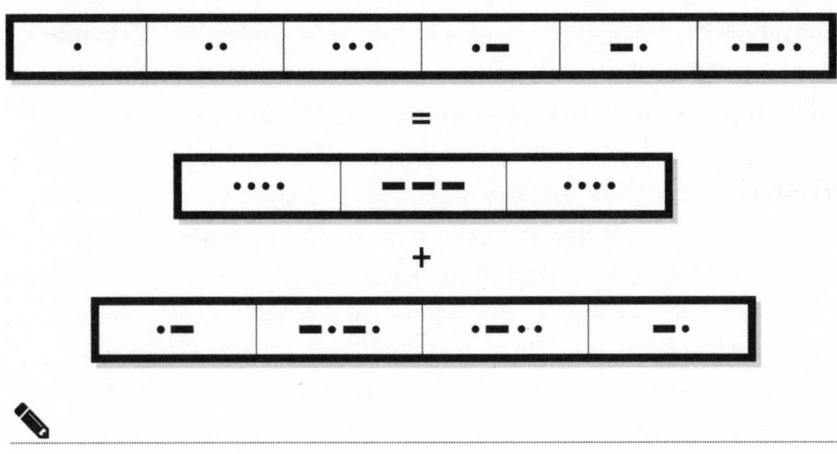

SOLUTIONS PAGE 209

SPECIAL FORCES

Since the time of the Greek city states, imperial armies had been disdainful of irregular warfare. Marching thousands of troops to their inevitable death was perfectly acceptable; breaking the rules of war, on the other hand, was not. This conservatism persisted into the Second World War, where many commanders still took a dim view of saboteurs and skirmishers.

However, empires of the modern era could not ignore the efficacy of the guerrilla tactics used against them by numerically inferior forces. The British Empire had learned a lot from fighting Afrikaners in the Boer Wars of 1880 and 1899. The expert marksmanship and fieldcraft of the Boer kommandos inspired the British to create their own elite units. They even borrowed the name.

Churchill called for a force of 5,000 volunteers to be specially trained for covert raiding expeditions against coastal targets. Their new methods of assault included both amphibious and parachute landings.

The commando training school was based at Achnacarry Castle in the Scottish Highlands. Throughout the war, men and women from all areas of the British Armed Forces were trained there, along with volunteers from allied nations, including the United States, who used the programme as a template for its own Army Rangers.

The first large-scale commando raid was Operation 'Claymore' in March 1941. A surprise attack on supplies and shipping in occupied Norway, it resulted in the capture of 228 enemy soldiers, the sinking of 10 ships and the destruction of glycerine production facilities used to make explosives. It was the first of a dozen such raids that forced the Nazis to grudgingly redeploy front-line troops to protect their assets.

The success of Operation 'Claymore' was widely publicized and a much-needed boost to British morale. It also yielded an invaluable prize that could not be shared with the public: a set of Enigma machine rotors and codebooks. These were promptly passed on to the codebreakers at Bletchley Park.

PUZZLE 95

To unlock this safe, all 20 buttons must be pressed in the correct order, finishing with the one marked OPEN. **What is the first button you must press?**

2D	2R	2L	1D
2R	2D	3D	2L
2D	1R	**OPEN**	2L
2R	1L	3U	1U
3R	4U	1L	1U

PUZZLE 96

Place a mine into some of the empty cells so that each number represents the total count of mines in neighbouring cells, including diagonally adjacent cells.

			2	1				2
	3						4	
3		2	1		3		3	
					2			
2		3				1		
2		3			2			3
		3	2				3	
2	3		3		2	2		
		2		1			3	2

SOLUTIONS PAGE 210

THE SOE

The commandos harassed the fringes of Nazi-occupied Europe, but Britain still lacked the strength and resources to strike any deeper. Once again, it would take a leaf from an enemy's book; in this case the Irish Republican Army, who had been waging a clandestine war against Britain since 1919.

In July 1940, a new, top-secret department of the Ministry of Economic Warfare was created: the Special Operations Executive (SOE). The SOE combined various agencies specializing in espionage, reconnaissance, sabotage and propaganda. Agents were sent to and recruited from German-occupied territories with the aim of doing as much damage to the Axis war effort as possible. Churchill ordered SOE chief Hugh Dalton to 'Set Europe ablaze!'

Agents from SOE's Section F were sent to occupied France where they would work in tandem with the French Resistance on a wide range of missions, including recruitment, intelligence gathering and sabotage. Many women were recruited as couriers and radio operators; these were extremely dangerous assignments and several female agents were captured, tortured and executed by the Nazi secret police, the Gestapo.

PUZZLE 97

Can you find five words or names relating to Second World War codebreaking hidden in the following lines? For example, the word 'spy' is hidden in the phrase 'victory is not in our gra<u>sp y</u>et'.

1. We need to make Ypres seem like the target of the operation.

2. We think the consul tracked us to this location.

3. The operation went from zero to roaring success in less than a week.

4. We found a crucial non-sequitur in German intelligence transcripts.

5. The machine turns a light bulb on if a certain letter is encrypted.

PUZZLE 98

The word search below contains the code names of 15 SOE networks. They may appear horizontally, vertically or diagonally, backwards or forwards. **Can you find them all?**

V	T	M	U	M	D	R	C	Z	F	Q	X	Y	S	X
I	S	O	S	C	I	E	N	T	I	S	T	G	M	H
Q	I	Y	J	L	Q	F	J	D	W	M	M	C	P	G
E	U	O	P	T	H	O	O	Z	A	G	G	H	T	H
P	Q	T	H	H	C	Q	I	R	Y	E	E	A	E	G
F	O	K	K	K	O	K	K	K	V	W	B	A	N	P
R	L	V	E	Q	U	S	D	I	C	O	D	U	R	H
E	I	Y	D	I	M	N	T	R	R	M	R	K	E	Y
E	R	D	W	A	R	C	D	C	A	C	X	N	K	S
L	T	T	N	B	E	L	A	S	H	Z	I	O	N	I
A	N	V	Z	T	T	J	T	I	N	O	I	M	I	C
N	E	V	E	A	M	E	N	I	C	J	D	W	T	I
C	V	D	Z	G	R	H	L	Y	J	H	Z	G	V	A
E	H	G	P	B	R	I	C	K	L	A	Y	E	R	N
L	T	C	H	W	N	N	H	F	W	D	C	J	D	E

The list of code names has been encrypted using the Atbash cipher.

ZXILYZG
YIRXPOZBVI
XRMVNZ
WVGVXGREV
UIVVOZMXV
SVZWNZHGVI
QLXPVB
NZIPHNZM
NLMP
KSBHRXRZM
HXRVMGRHG
GRMPVI
FIXSRM
EVMGIROLJFRHG
DRAZIW

SOLUTIONS PAGE 211

The Secret Intelligence Service was also responsible for intelligence gathering in the occupied territories and often locked horns with the SOE, which it saw as 'amateurish' and dangerously cavalier with its penchant for blowing things up. Nevertheless, the combined efforts of the SOE and expanding Resistance networks gave the people hope that liberation might someday be possible.

The situation in Czechoslovakia was somewhat different than France – its resistance movement was small and its people, for the most part, subdued. The Reich Protector of Bohemia and Moravia, SS-Obergruppenführer Reinhard Heydrich, was one of Hitler's most trusted supporters and a brutally efficient dictator himself. In May 1942, the SOE assassinated Heydrich, which led to bloody reprisals against the population – around 1,300 Czechoslovaks were executed. This ignited the resistance movement in the country, albeit at a terrible cost.

The SOE also encouraged anti-Nazi activity in Yugoslavia and this resulted in a coup d'état in 1941. The victory proved to be pyrrhic, however; the Axis subsequently invaded and occupied the country and went on to conquer Greece for good measure. Hitler's domination of continental Europe was almost complete, but his belief in his own infallibility would soon be tested.

PUZZLE 99

Can you decrypt this message to discover an agency's headquarters?

QAXTYOJUP HSDLP QTPLLT

CLUE (Atbash): UZNLFH URXGRLMZO WVGVXGREV

THE TURN OF THE TIDE

The pact between the Third Reich and the Soviet Union was nothing more than a ploy that allowed both countries to partition Poland. Hitler had always been vocal in both his contempt for communism and his desire to expand German *Lebensraum* into the Russian steppes.

Although the Soviet Red Army was formidable in terms of manpower, Stalin's paranoia had devastated it – almost three-quarters of its senior commanders had been imprisoned or executed. Stalin knew that Hitler could not be trusted but was determined to hold on to peace for as long as possible.

However, on 22 June 1941, Hitler ended the charade and launched Operation 'Barbarossa' – the invasion of the Soviet Union.

THE EASTERN FRONT

'Barbarossa' would open up the largest theatre of war in history – a clash of men and machines on an unprecedented scale, with atrocities and a loss of life that would dwarf even those of the First World War.

It was a three-pronged attack, targeting Leningrad in the north, Moscow in the centre and Ukraine, with its vital oilfields, in the south. Hitler planned to use Blitzkrieg to strike deep into Soviet territory before the full might of the Red Army could be brought to bear.

Many commanders had reservations about the plan but none had the courage to defy Hitler. An obvious issue was the scale of the operation – the Soviet Union covered an area well over twice the size of Europe. However, the operation started well; the Luftwaffe was able to secure total air superiority, while Panzers sped across the plains capturing town after town and hundreds of thousands of Soviet prisoners.

SOLUTIONS PAGE 212

What could have been a formidable victory, however, was hampered by a number of factors, not least of which was Hitler's interference. Contradicting the tactical sense of competent commanders, like Heinz Guderian, led to a number of delays and missed opportunities.

While thousands of their countrymen died from starvation and the Panzers raced towards Moscow, the Red Army began to rally. They also upgraded their technology: their T-34 tanks were better armed and better able to handle the terrain than the German Panzer IVs. Nevertheless, the Wehrmacht still had numerical superiority in both airpower and armoured fighting vehicles, and its well-disciplined troops were more than a match for the Red Army.

But a new enemy entered the fight the Germans had not prepared for: the weather.

First came the rain, turning rich farmland into soaking mud. This had been the nemesis of Blitzkrieg on the Western Front; now it brought the assault on the Soviet capital to a squelching halt.

But the rain was a mere inconvenience compared to the Russian winter. Blinding snow and lethal sub-zero winds battered the invaders, who had neglected to bring appropriate seasonal clothing. Even the fuel froze, making the German Panzers impotent. The invaders were forced to dig in and wait.

Hitler was furious. He fired his senior officers and assumed direct command of the invasion. With the spring thaw, he turned his attention to the southern oilfields, a logical strategic objective. Hitler then made another inexplicable miscalculation: he diverted a significant portion of his forces to attack a nearby city that happened to bear his hated foe's name.

Stalingrad would become synonymous with the savagery of urban warfare. The Soviets had effectively fortified the city and were determined to hold it against the Nazis. The attackers hit it with everything they had – Stukas, artillery, stormtroopers – until it barely resembled a city at all. But even in the blackened ruins, the defenders continued to resist, moving like ghosts through the sewers and sniping with deadly accuracy from the shadows of burnt-out buildings. Nevertheless, German victory seemed assured, and a final push sent in Panzers to engage the entrenched survivors at point-blank range, taking block after block of the city.

But Stalin had become as obsessed with his namesake as Hitler. He ordered a secret massive mobilization to reinforce Stalingrad. The Germans were suddenly overwhelmed and surrounded. Those who did not surrender proposed a tactical withdrawal. But Hitler refused to sanction it. Attempts to rescue the trapped Wehrmacht troops were repelled by the Soviets and most of the airdropped supplies failed to reach them.

The Russian winter returned, adding frostbite to the list of German woes. Finally, they were forced to surrender. Stalingrad had cost the Axis dearly. Some 800,000 Germans were killed, wounded or captured, and for the first time, the Wehrmacht was made to look weak.

The Germans then began a general retreat. Although they had suffered devastating losses, they were able to withdraw in good order. Hitler, however, was not happy with the retrograde action and decided to launch a new offensive: Operation 'Citadel'.
To counter the threat of the Russian T-34s, a new generation of German Panzers was spawned: the Tiger. But the Germans had lost the initiative, and the Red Army was now wise to Blitzkrieg. At the Battle of Kursk, Hitler received another humiliating lesson from the Red Army, losing thousands more men, hundreds of tanks and any remaining hope of taking *Lebensraum* from Russia.

PUZZLE 100

Leopold is only half as good as Charles but ten times better than Victor.

Douglas is only half as good as Maurice but five times better than Charles.

Victor is only half as good as Xavier. **Is he better than Ivan?**

SOLUTIONS PAGE 212

THE PACIFIC

By declaring war on the Soviet Union, Hitler had given Great Britain an unexpected break. Churchill seized the opportunity and opened talks with Moscow.

The United States had been providing Britain with supplies without breaking its neutral status. This suited Hitler who had no immediate plans to embroil the Americans. But on a bright Sunday morning on 7 December 1941, everything changed. Japan launched an attack against the US naval base at Pearl Harbor in Hawaii.

The attack came without warning. Japan had not formally declared war on the United States or even informed its Axis partners of the plan. It hoped to cripple its rival's naval power so it could pursue its imperialist ambitions in the Pacific without interference.

After two hours of relentless bombardment, over 2,000 Americans were dead and four of their eight battleships had been sunk. The operation was only a partial success, however, as the United States' two aircraft carriers were not in port at the time of the attack.

The United States Congress declared war on Japan, after an address by President Roosevelt the following day. The two other primary Axis powers, Germany and Italy, then declared war on the US. Again, Hitler dismissed warnings from his military advisors that Germany was overextending itself.

PUZZLE 101

Can you decrypt this quote?

SDKXWWRMUHGMDLVMNESRANPEEY

CLUE (Atbash): QZKZMVHV IRXV DRMV

Japan, who viewed the Americans as decadent and having no stomach for war, believed it had neutralized the United States. It then began a ruthless campaign against the western colonies in Asia, invading Thailand and Malaya and removing the British Indian troops stationed there. Then it made its way south

CODEBREAKERS

The Second World War saw a cryptographical arms race, as intelligence divisions on both sides sought to build uncrackable codes – while the enemy busied themselves with cracking them. Can you identify the machines below, and ascertain which is the odd one out?

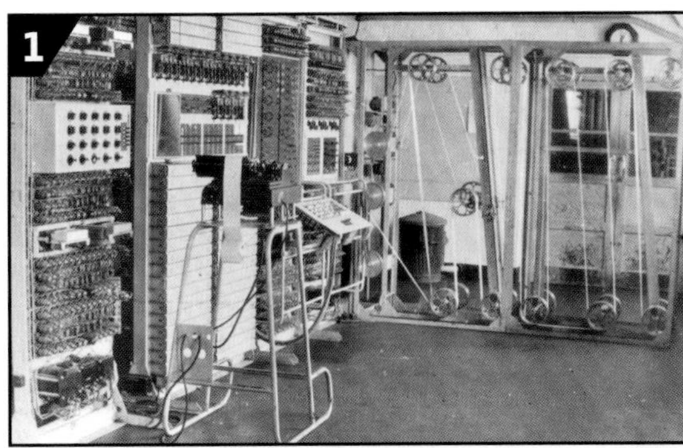

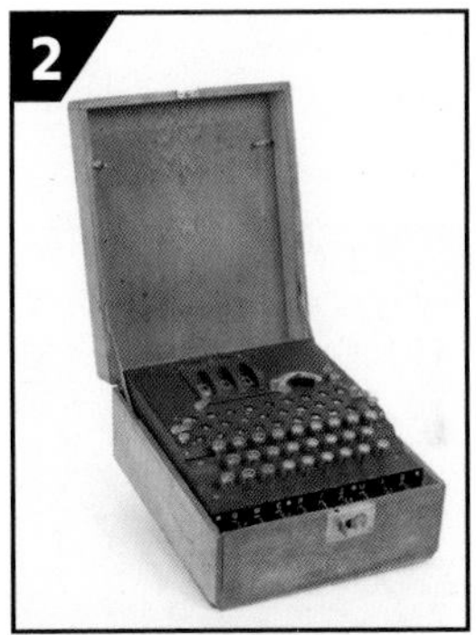

SOLUTIONS PAGE 30

THE SECOND WORLD WAR AT SEA

The five battleships below each belonged to different nations. Can you match the names to the image? Next, can you discover the link between them, and which battleship is the odd one out?

1

2

Battleships:
USS *Arizona*,
HMS *Barham*,
***Bismarck*,**
***Roma*,**
Yamato

SOLUTIONS PAGE 30

BATTLES OF THE SECOND WORLD WAR

Each of these battles or operations began in a different year during the Second World War. From just these images, can you name each battle and which year it began in?

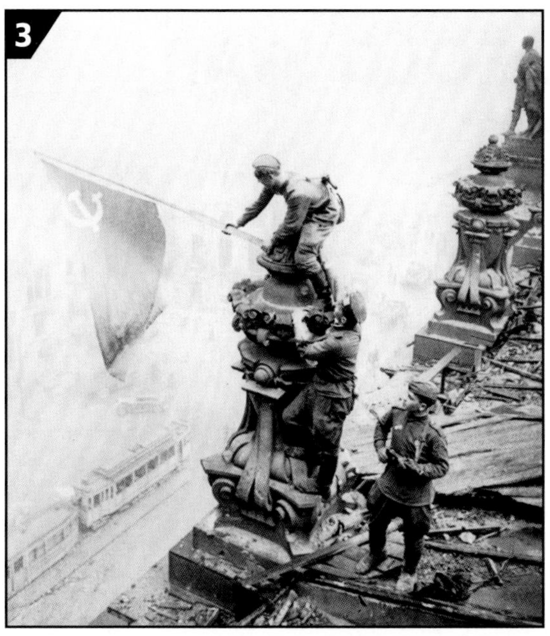

Years:
1940,
1941,
1942,
1944,
1945

SOLUTIONS PAGE 30

CRUCIAL COLD WAR MOMENTS

The Cold War was a long period in which not all that much happened in terms of direct military engagement between the superpowers, punctuated by moments of high tension and peril. Can you identify the four events represented by the images below and thus discover the odd one out?

1

2

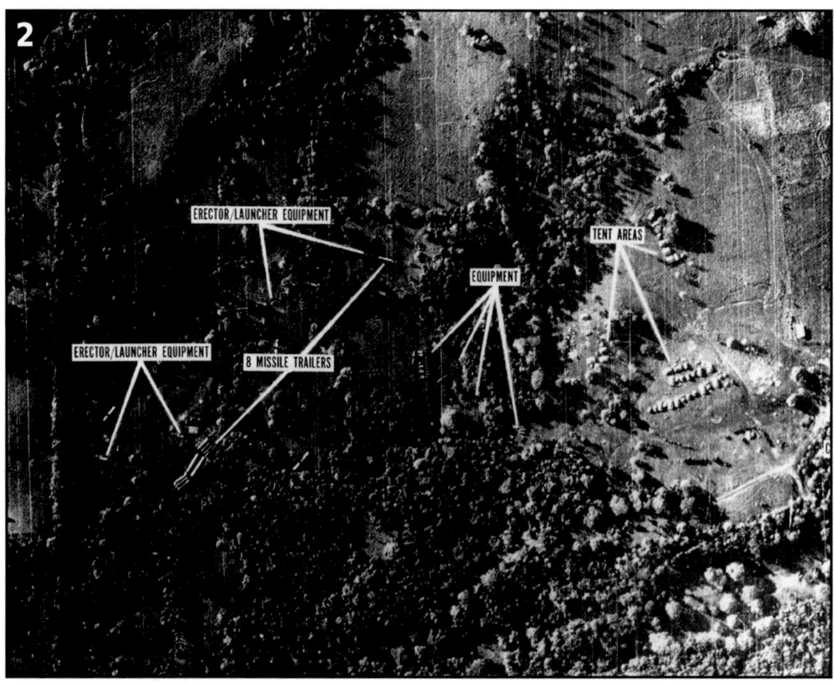

SOLUTIONS PAGE 30

SOVIET ESPIONAGE IN THE COLD WAR

The Cold War allowed the art of espionage to reach new heights. Below are six people associated with Soviet espionage. Can you name each individual, the name of the group they are most affiliated with, and identify the odd one out?

SOLUTIONS PAGE 30

HEATING UP WITH PROXY WARS

Although the Cold War, fortunately, never evolved into the Third World War, a number of proxy wars were fought with varying levels of involvement from each of the superpowers. Can you identify the five wars from the images? The conflicts spanned the entire Cold War, and their dates are provided below as clues: Image 1 – 1955–1975; Image 2 – 1946–1954; Image 3 – 1979–1989; Image 4 – 1974–2002; Image 5 – 1950–1953.

1

2

3

4

5

SOLUTIONS PAGE 30

LEADERS THROUGH THE YEARS

The Cold War was 'fought' with high-level diplomacy as much as it was with espionage and proxy wars. Personal relationships were all important. A path can be drawn between the six leaders pictured using the five meetings listed – one of the pictures even shows two of the leaders at the summit; the answer for that image is the waving Russian leader. Can you name the leaders and follow the path of meetings between them from first to last?

Meetings:
5th G7 Summit,
9th G7 Summit,
Geneva Summit,
Strategic Arms Limitation Treaty II (SALT II),
Washington/ Camp David Summit

SOLUTIONS PAGE 30

SOLUTIONS

CODEBREAKERS

1. Colossus Computer
2. Enigma Machine
3. Typex Machine
4. Combined Cipher Machine
5. Lorenz Cipher

The odd one out is the Colossus Computer. The other four were all used to encrypt messages. The Colossus was built by the Bletchley Park codebreakers to crack encryptions.

THE SECOND WORLD WAR AT SEA

1. *Bismarck*
2. HMS *Barham*
3. *Roma*
4. USS *Arizona*
5. *Yamato*

Each of these battleships was sunk over the course of the Second World War with great loss of life. The odd one out is the USS *Arizona*. The other battleships were all sunk while out at sea, whereas the USS *Arizona* was bombed by the Japanese while at Pearl Harbor.

BATTLES OF THE SECOND WORLD WAR

1. Battle of Crete (1941)
2. Operation Overlord/D-Day (1944)
3. Battle of Berlin (1945)
4. Battle of Stalingrad (1942)
5. Battle of France (1940)

CRUCIAL COLD WAR MOMENTS

1. The U-2 Incident – pictured is a Lockheed U-2 spy plane.
2. The Cuban Missile Crisis – this is a US reconnaissance photo of the Soviet missile site at Mariel Naval Port, Cuba, 8 November 1962.
3. The Sputnik Crisis – this is a photograph of a replica of Sputnik 1, the first artificial satellite to be put into orbit in outer space.
4. The fall of the Berlin Wall – in this photograph, East German guards struggle to restrain a crowd of East Berliners at one of the checkpoints along the Berlin Wall.

The fall of the Berlin Wall is the odd one out, because it is the only event that is not known as a crisis. All of the others were moments of great peril, whereas the fall of the Wall led to the end of the Cold War.

SOVIET ESPIONAGE IN THE COLD WAR

1. Joseph McCarthy – McCarthyism
2. Julius and Ethel Rosenberg – Atomic Spies
3. Harry Dexter White – Silvermaster Spy Ring
4. Kim Philby – Cambridge Five
5. Lona Cohen – Portland Spy Ring

The odd one out is Joseph McCarthy. All of the others were Soviet spies, whereas McCarthy made his career out of seeing far more communist spies than there really were.

HEATING UP WITH PROXY WARS

1. Vietnam War
2. First Indochina War
3. Soviet–Afghan War
4. Angolan Civil War
5. Korean War

LEADERS THROUGH THE YEARS

The leaders are Margaret Thatcher, Leonid Brezhnev, George H.W. Bush, Mikhail Gorbachev, Jimmy Carter, Ronald Reagan. The correct pathway is:
2. Leonid Brezhnev – **5.** Jimmy Carter – Strategic Arms Limitation Treaty II
5. Jimmy Carter – **1.** Margaret Thatcher – 5th G7 Summit
1. Margaret Thatcher – **6.** Ronald Reagan– 9th G7 Summit
6. Ronald Reagan – **4.** Mikhail Gorbachev – Geneva Summit
4. Mikhail Gorbachev – **3.** George H.W. Bush – Washington/Camp David Summit.

THE ALBERTI CIPHER WHEEL

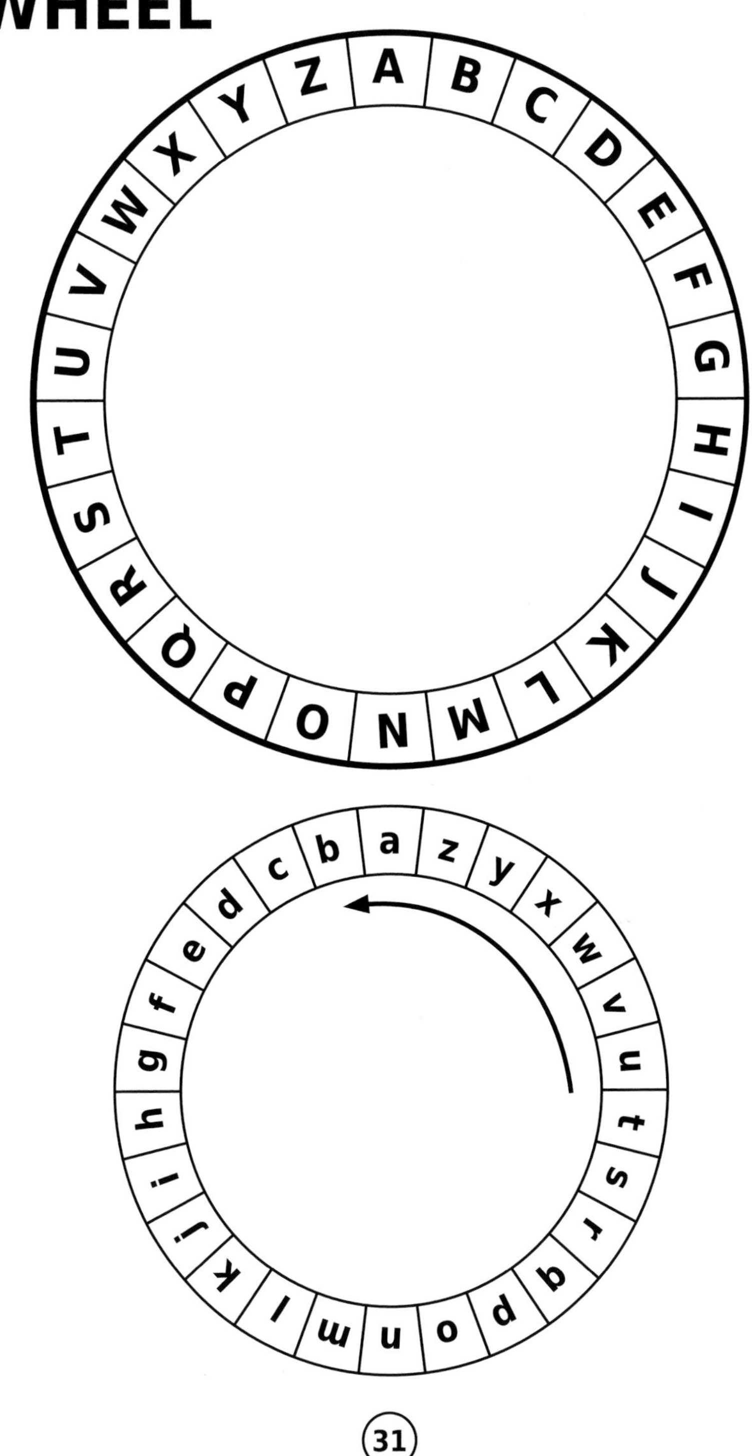

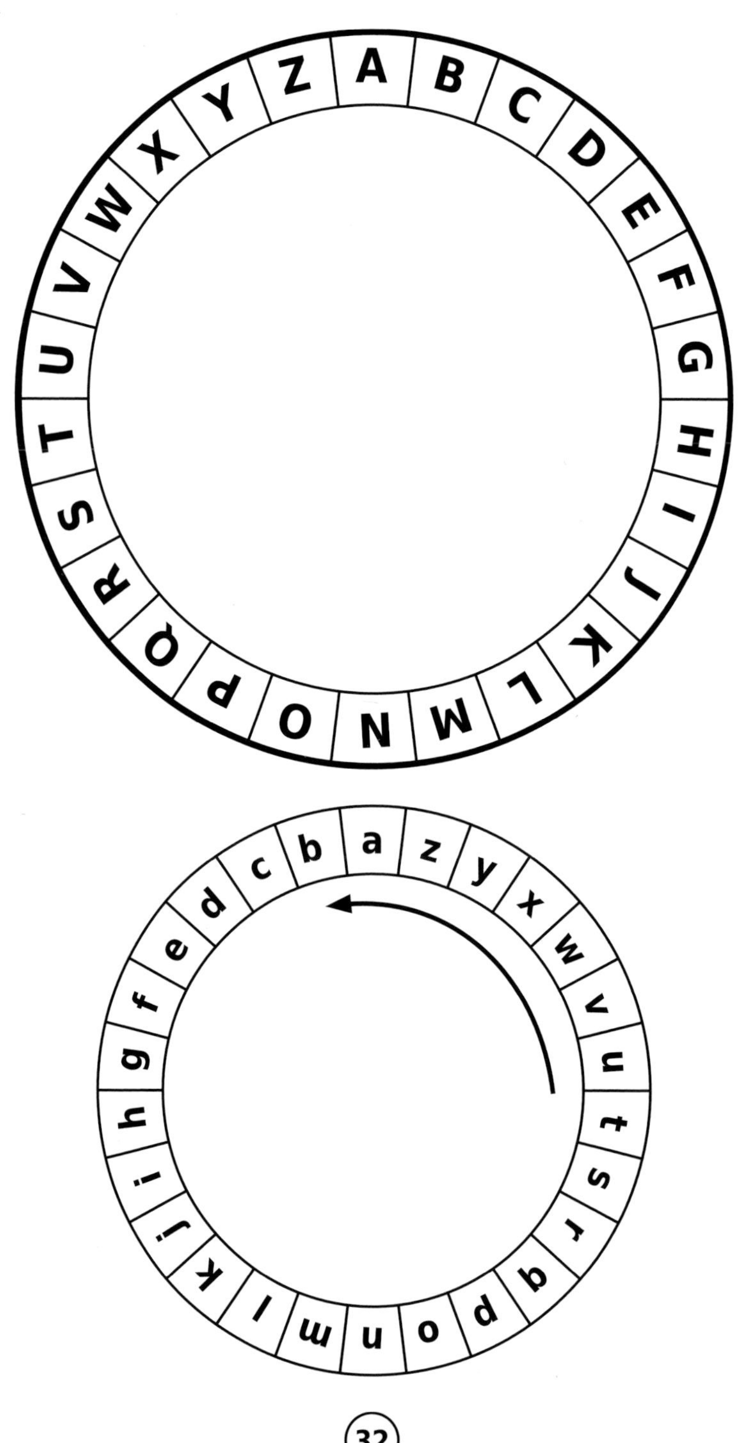
A B C D E F G H I J K L M N O P Q R S T U V W X Y Z
a z y x w v u t s r q p o n m l k j i h g f e d c b

towards Singapore, the heart of Britain's colonial influence in the region. The British massively underestimated the Japanese and suffered humiliating defeats on land, sea and in the air. Singapore was forced to surrender, and some 80,000 British, Australian and Indian troops were taken prisoner.

Further disasters followed with Hong Kong, the Philippines (an American protectorate) and Burma falling to the Japanese. They now seemed to be the undisputed masters of the Pacific, but they had badly misjudged the American response to their aggression.

Four months after Pearl Harbor, the surviving US aircraft carriers launched the Doolittle Raid – named after the USAAF Colonel who led it – dropping bombs on Tokyo and other major cities. This was a largely symbolic and morale-boosting venture, but it still made Japan realize that to protect its homeland it would have to create a defensive perimeter by occupying a number of Pacific islands, including Australia. America was forewarned, having successfully broken the enemy's naval encryption, and immediately mobilized to prevent this from happening.

May 1942 saw the first major naval engagement between carrier fleets in the Battle of the Coral Sea. Unlike previous battleship-centred engagements, which had been fought at relatively close range, this new type of warfare saw fighters and bombers operating beyond the fleets' lines of sight. Although both sides suffered equal losses, the battle prevented Japan from invading Australia.

The following month, Japan made a desperate gamble by attacking Midway Island, located roughly halfway between North America and Asia. The plan consisted of an elaborate feint to draw away some of the defenders, but US signals intelligence exposed the ruse and turned the tables on the attackers. Japan suffered a catastrophic loss that should have put an end to its dreams of Pacific supremacy.

Unfortunately, it would take far more to quell Japan's determination. Its army and air force possessed a fanatical loyalty born out of the ancient warrior code *bushido*. Death in battle was always preferable to the ignominy of surrender. But they now faced a United States whose war economy had gone into overdrive. The battle for the Pacific would rage for another three years.

SOLUTIONS PAGE 212

PUZZLE 102

Battleships! Find the enemy fleet on the grid below. The numbers on the periphery tell you how many occupied squares are in that row or column. No two vessels occupy neighbouring squares (including diagonals). There are four kinds of vessel and the number of each type in the fleet is as follows:

Battleship	◀■■▶	x1	**Destroyer**	◀▶	x3
Cruiser	◀■▶	x2	**Submarine**	■	x4

	0	6	0	2	3	1	1	2	5	0	
0											0
2											2
3								◀			3
2											2
3											3
0											0
3						■					3
2									◀		2
2				◀							2
3											3
	0	6	0	2	3	1	1	2	5	0	

THE MEDITERRANEAN

Benito Mussolini had ambitions every bit as grand as those of his fellow Axis leaders. He dreamed of a new Roman Empire that would encompass the Mediterranean and most of North Africa.

His fully modernized navy already challenged British sea power in the region and threatened its access to oil from the Middle East.

Italy controlled the North African nations of Libya and Abyssinia, which were separated from one another by British-occupied Egypt and Sudan. Given that his troops outnumbered the British by almost ten to one, an invasion of these countries seemed a mere formality.

Mussolini certainly had no shortage of confidence but his attention to detail was questionable. The Italian army had a morale problem, possibly stemming from the relatively poor quality of its officers, who lacked the fanatical ideology of the Nazis and Japanese.

The Italian invasion of Egypt was not only repelled – the British pursued the attackers back into Libya and took over 100,000 prisoners. After almost a year of fighting, they also took Abyssinia and sent reinforcements across the Mediterranean to help Greece, who was successfully repelling its own Italian invaders.

Mussolini was no Julius Caesar; in fact, he was proving to be something of an embarrassment for the Axis, so Hitler begrudgingly sent his own forces into the Balkans in an effort to regain control.

The combined might of the Wehrmacht and the allied Italian army was too much for the Greek, British, Australian and New Zealand defenders. After overrunning mainland Greece, Hitler took the island of Crete with a large force of *fallschirmjäger* (paratroopers). Despite this success, Hitler was aghast at the number of troops he had lost and discontinued the strategy of mass airborne assault. The Allies, however, saw the potential of paratroopers and went on to train their own elite regiments.

Greece was completely occupied by the Axis in April 1941. It was a particularly brutal occupation – tens of thousands of civilians were murdered and many starved to death. But the Greek Resistance was one of the strongest in Europe, and they would make their unwanted guests pay a heavy price for their stay.

PUZZLE 103

What English word starts with an 'E' and ends with an 'E' but only contains a single letter?

SOLUTIONS PAGE 212

PUZZLE 104

Decrypt this quote. Who said it, and when?

JIZCNMBLAFDYXJLLBLFUEUYXRGOFVPA
DFCZXRRVQWOWITWVMVXDEODND
FQCMSDZYJMLCLAIUFIKHECWWAVB

CLUE (Atbash): GSIVV GDL LMV

Having taken control of the Balkans, Hitler turned his attention to North Africa, sending ace Panzer commander Erwin Rommel and his *Afrika Korps* to crush the depleted Allied forces in Libya. After initial successes, the Germans began to overextend their supply lines. The Allies counter-attacked, pushing the invaders back until they too became exhausted. This back-and-forth across the desert went on for months, to the consternation of both Hitler and Churchill.

Despite numerous German attempts to knock out the strategically important island of Malta, its garrison and civilian population held firm and it remained under British control. Mussolini's much-vaunted navy could not maintain control of the Mediterranean either. Once again, Hitler was forced to divert his military to the region.

The turning point in the battle for North Africa came in October 1942 near the Egyptian town of El Alamein. A new commander, Bernard Montgomery, was appointed to lead an Eighth Army offensive against Rommel's Panzers. He received some much-needed supplies and reinforcements, including new M4 Sherman tanks from the United States. For the first time in the campaign, the Allies had a tank that was a match for the Panzer IV. Montgomery was also assured of his numerical advantage (essential when attacking well-entrenched defenders) from intelligence supplied by Ultra.

Things were less positive for the Germans. Rommel's supplies were running low and reinforcements unlikely since the Wehrmacht was tied up fighting the Soviet Union. Nevertheless, he defended his position well – despite being in ill health – and took a terrible toll on the attackers. But in the end, he was forced to retreat. This was the first major victory by Western Allied forces and provided a huge morale boost, paving the way for more successes, which ultimately drove the Axis out of Africa.

After asserting control of North Africa and much of the Mediterranean, the Allies returned their attention to the occupied Balkans and Italy. Although the British were starting to gain the upper hand, they had not forgotten the value of deception either and came up with two ingenious ruses.

The first was Operation 'Barclay' – the creation of a completely fictitious army, supposedly preparing for an assault via the Balkans. The second, Operation 'Mincemeat', was even more devious.

On 30 April 1943, the corpse of Royal Marines Captain (acting Major) William Martin washed up on the coast of Spain. On his body were two items of personal correspondence from more senior officials – he was a courier – indicating that the Allies had intended to attack Greece and Crete but, fearing the German defences were too strong, would now attack Sardinia instead. The Spanish passed this vital intelligence to the Abwehr who then ensured that troops were sent to reinforce the 'real' targets.

Unfortunately for the Axis, the late captain was in fact a homeless Welshman by the name of Glyndwr Michael who had died tragically after ingesting rat poison. He had been dressed as an officer and provided with completely fake documents. The Allies' real target was Sicily.

The successful invasion of Sicily was the final straw for Mussolini. After a vote in the Italian Grand Council, he was dismissed and immediately arrested on the orders of King Victor Emmanuel III, bringing an end to his fascist dictatorship. Hitler was again forced to divert his forces to keep control of the mainland as British and American forces moved in. The German defence was tenacious. It was not until June 1944 that the Allies were able to break through and liberate Rome, and it took almost another year to push the Nazi forces out of Italy altogether.

SOLUTIONS PAGE 213

THE ROAD TO VICTORY

America's entry into the war on 7 December 1941 was a critical turning point. It brought a halt to Japanese expansion in the Pacific and a ray of hope to occupied Europe. Hitler had overplayed his hand on the Eastern Front and in the Mediterranean and was now forced to defend his conquests closer to home.

His plan to starve Britain out of the war by attacking its Atlantic supply convoys had been brutally effective. But by 1943 advances in anti-submarine technology had culled the U-Boat 'wolfpacks'. With this threat removed, the US was free to send reinforcements, armaments and supplies across the ocean.

DESTRUCTION

The US Army Air Force and RAF began a combined bombing offensive in 1943, including the controversial 'strategic' bombing of population centres such as Hamburg and Dresden. Tens of thousands of civilians were killed or made homeless by the campaign but, as with the Blitz, it did little to dampen the morale of the people.

PUZZLE 105

Although the Germans had a functioning air defence network, a new innovation had been developed to protect Allied bombers, code-named 'Window'. **What was it?**

On the Eastern Front, the Wehrmacht was being annihilated. Hitler, however, would not tolerate any more withdrawals. The Germans had no choice but to disobey him, as torrents of T-34s, fresh from the Soviet war factories, surged on all fronts and partisans nipped at their heels. After each retreat, Hitler would sack and replace commanding officers, only for the pattern to be repeated. The Nazis continued to take savage reprisals against the Soviets and destroyed everything of value as they retreated through Russia and the Ukraine.

The Red Army was relentless (also invading Finland and forcing its surrender while barely breaking stride) and continued to push the Wehrmacht back through Belarus and into Poland. With victory in sight, Stalin changed his objectives – he would crush Germany only after he had annexed the 'liberated' East European states to his own communist empire.

In Poland's capital Warsaw, the underground resistance movement, encouraged by the advance of the Red Army, initiated an uprising against the retreating Germans. But Stalin ordered his forces to halt outside the city thus allowing the Germans to regroup, massacre thousands of Poles and reduce their capital to rubble.

Only when the last remnants of pro-Western resistance had been obliterated did the Russians move in. Poland would be added to a list of Soviet buffer states that Stalin had secretly agreed with Churchill. Both leaders now turned acquisitive eyes to the rest of Europe, even while they raced to stop Germany.

SOLUTIONS PAGE 213

PUZZLE 106

Here is an encrypted version of an informal agreement made between Churchill and Stalin at the Moscow Conference in October 1944. **Can you decrypt it?**

	ORPPCN	AOCQNCJ
OKINJCN	90	10
YOHHUH	90	10
XRYKPFNSCN	50	50
BRJYNOX	50	50
ARFYNOCN	75	25

CLUE (Atbash): MZFTSGB

LIBERATION

Hitler knew the Allies were preparing to invade Western Europe, but with many of his troops struggling to hold back the Soviet onslaught and the Allied advance in the Mediterranean, he could not defend every potential invasion point at once. He had already ordered the construction of an Atlantic Wall on 23 March 1942, covering almost 2,700 kilometres of coastline, with giant gun emplacements at key defensive locations. Now, Field Marshal Rommel was ordered to inspect the wall and issue orders for its strengthening. Hitler planned to be well prepared for any and every potential invasion.

For their part, the Allies knew that a direct amphibious assault on a well-defended German fortification would be tantamount to suicide. The invasion of Europe, code-named Operation 'Overlord', would require meticulous planning, as well as good intelligence and counter-intelligence.

Roosevelt and Churchill agreed that 'Overlord' should commence in summer 1944. Two possible invasion points were proposed: the Pas de Calais and Normandy. The former was the better option since it was closer to both Britain and to Germany. This also made it the more obvious choice, so they opted for the latter.

An elaborate deception campaign, code-named 'Bodyguard', used the German spies who had been turned by *Double-Cross* to feed false information back to German High Command. The Allies also created a fake US Army group, stationed just across from the Pas de Calais, complete with fake tanks, aircraft and assault transports. The Germans took the bait.

The invasion (D-Day) began on 6 June 1944. The morning sky over Normandy was suddenly filled with paratroopers. The paratroopers were the first to set foot in Nazi-occupied France and began securing key bridges in the region. This was followed by a ferocious coastal bombardment from Allied battleships and aircraft. Then came the most perilous phase: waves of American, British and Canadian landing craft surged towards the beaches under a relentless German artillery barrage. Those that made it unleashed assault troops who were further subjected to intense machine-gun fire. They sustained horrendous casualties but, in defiance of the odds, eventually secured a foothold.

SOLUTIONS PAGE 213

Hitler, still acting on falsified intelligence, did not immediately authorize reinforcements to the region. He still believed the invasion was a feint. This bought the Allies time to get the remainder of their troops and armour ashore. But they now had to navigate the difficult Normandy countryside as they made their way inland and the fighting intensified. The Germans were using their most advanced tanks – the Tiger series – which made mincemeat of the much lighter (and more flammable) Shermans. Furthermore, among the multitude of soldiers defending in Normandy were the Nazis' most fanatical troops, the Waffen-SS, who were deployed to repel the attack and defended with a tenacity that turned every town and village the Allies entered into a miniature Stalingrad.

The Allied breakout came at great cost, but it was finally achieved thanks to effective planning, determination and air support. Once again, Hitler's contribution cannot be understated – his stubborn refusal to listen to (or retain) his best military advisors greatly assisted the Allied cause. Another failed attempt on his life by senior officers heightened his paranoia and made his decisions increasingly erratic. Against his wishes, the German occupying forces fell back, and town after town fell to the Allies.

As the US 3rd Army under George Patton raced towards Paris, the French Resistance initiated a massive armed uprising and the Germans were forced to surrender. This was no coincidence; the actions of the Resistance were coordinated specifically by the 2nd French Armoured Division of the Free French Forces to occur simultaneously with the attack on Paris.

Charles de Gaulle returned to his liberated capital on 25 August 1944. With France freed from Nazi occupation, the Allies prepared for a final push into Germany itself.

PUZZLE 107

Shade the cells so that each number represents the total number of shaded cells touching that cell, including diagonally, and including itself. Is anything revealed?

			2		1	1	0			1
2	4	3		3		1		2		
1		1	2	1	1	0	1	1	2	1
2	4	2			2	0	2	3	4	2
	2		2	1	1		1		2	1
	4		4	2	1		3			2
1	2	2		1			2	2	2	
3	4		3	3		3			3	1
2	2	2	1			2	2		1	
			1		2	2	2	1	1	
1	1	0								

SOLUTIONS PAGE 214

VENGEANCE

With the Western Allies and Soviets closing in on Germany, Hitler became desperate. He ordered long-range strikes against the British mainland with his new 'Vengeance Weapons', the V1 and V2. Once again London was savagely bombarded. The relentless attacks would only cease once the Allies had pushed the German mobile launchers out of range.

In September 1944, the Allies liberated Belgium, but they were encountering increasing German resistance and their advance started to slow. They still had many miles to cover before they would confront an even greater obstacle: Germany's fortified Siegfried Line.

An ambitious plan by Field Marshal Bernard Montgomery hoped to speed up the offensive by using a combination of airborne and ground troops to seize key bridges and create a corridor into Arnhem in German-occupied Holland. If successful, it would enable the Allies to bypass the Siegfried Line and strike into Germany from the north. Unfortunately, Operation 'Market Garden', as it was known, was a failure and diminished the prospect of ending the war quickly.

The port of Antwerp was the Allies' next target. If the well-defended estuary leading to the port could be taken, it would open up a sea route for supplies and reinforcements. The First Canadian Army led the mission with a series of amphibious and ground assaults. They endured terrible losses but eventually secured the vital objective and reinforcements began to arrive in ever-greater numbers.

PUZZLE 108

Each letter of the alphabet has been encrypted to a number (1 to 26). Crack the code to solve the puzzle and reveal two operational words. To start you off, the codes for three letters have been given.

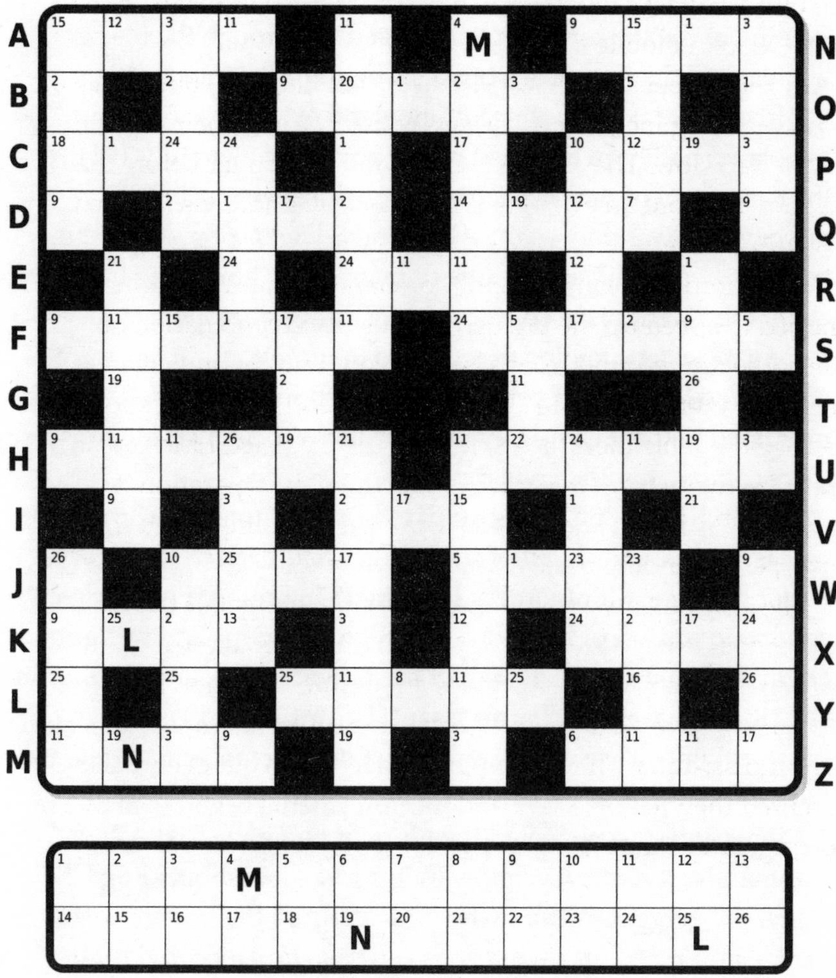

SOLUTIONS PAGE 214

Hitler ordered Antwerp to be retaken and threw almost all of his reserves into a surprise counteroffensive on 16 December 1944. The outnumbered Americans who were defending the Ardennes region were caught completely off guard and forced to withdraw. However, their lines did not break, they simply 'bulged'. The ensuing Battle of the Bulge saw some of the most desperate fighting of the Western Front and raged on through the bleak winter until the Americans broke through on 25 January 1945.

Although Majdanek concentration and extermination camp, in Poland, had been liberated by the Soviet Army in July 1944, the true extent of the Nazi's barbaric actions were still largely unknown. It was only as the Allies and Soviets approached the heart of the Third Reich did the unimaginably horrifying truth about the Nazi's plans come to light. Death camps created for the systematic extermination of Jews and other 'undesirables' were discovered. Millions of prisoners had been secretly brutalized and murdered in these camps, even while the war claimed millions more combatants and civilians.

In March 1945, the Allies prepared to cross the Rhine; this was no easy feat as almost all of the bridges had been destroyed on Hitler's orders. Montgomery launched Operation 'Plunder', a combined assault of bombers, amphibious troops and bridge engineers from the west bank of the Lower Rhine, and Operation 'Varsity', a massive airborne assault by British and American paratroopers on the enemy side. Despite a stoic German defence, the bridgehead was secured.

Montgomery was denied the glory of being the first Allied commander to enter Germany by his rival, swashbuckling US General George S. Patton, who had captured the Ludendorff Bridge and raced his own troops across in advance of 'Plunder'.

This was the beginning of the end for the Nazis. While the Western Allies stormed across the Rhine, the Red Army was sweeping in from the east. Their First Army Group commander, Georgy Zhukov, gave the Wehrmacht a final devastating lesson in Blitzkrieg, then regrouped less than 80 kilometres from Berlin. The Western Allies had been instructed to focus on liberating the occupied territories, and they left the capital to the Soviets, who would mercilessly repay the Nazis for the misery inflicted on their homeland.

On 30 April 1945, Adolf Hitler, surrounded by the nightmare he had created, took his own life.

PUZZLE 109

Can you unscramble the code names of eight Second World War operations below, which have each had their letters jumbled up and some spaces introduced? One extra letter has been added to each name which, when all eight are extracted and read in order from top to bottom, will spell out a word relating to war.

RATED REMAKING ....

PRUNED NL ....

VENAL ....

BEIGE ARC ....

MANIC MEETS ....

ROD OR EVIL ....

TYRO VISA ....

OR A BRASS BAN ....

SOLUTIONS PAGE 215

After seven more days of desperate fighting, the Nazis gave their unconditional surrender, ending the war in Europe.

In the Pacific, the battle for the islands surrounding Japan continued. The US Army, Navy and Marines outnumbered the Japanese and were outfitted with superior military technology. But they faced a fanatical foe who would not contemplate surrender, making every engagement a bloodbath. The US no longer felt obliged to fight with thoughts of taking prisoners; instead, they bombed the islands ruthlessly and finished off the survivors with flamethrowers.

Despite horrendous losses, the Japanese became more incensed, launching deliberate suicide attacks, including the infamous kamikaze bombers.

The liberation of Burma, the Philippines and Malaya was eventually achieved after months of desperate ground combat, but the prospect of invading Japan itself remained a concern.

The first stepping stone was the enemy airbase on the island of Iwo Jima, some 1,200 km from the Japanese mainland. America had an overwhelming advantage in the assault planned for 19 February 1945 and their victory was almost assured. But the subsequent battle was one of the bloodiest of the Pacific campaign. The Japanese fought to the death and exacted a heavy price on the invaders – some 7,000 US marines killed and another 19,217 wounded, as per a Marine Corps monograph published in 1954.

A strategic bombing campaign was proposed to knock out Japanese military production and starve the nation into submission. Range was the key issue; the new B-29 'Superfortress' bombers could make the round trip to Tokyo but their fighter escorts could not. This meant the bombers had to operate at extremely high altitudes with a consequent loss of accuracy. Tokyo endured a relentless firebombing in March 1945 with tens of thousands of civilian casualties.

PUZZLE 110

Can you complete this Second World War-themed crossword? If you are struggling with some of the answers, reading the rest of this chapter might help.

ACROSS

1 6th June 1944 (1-3)
7 One of three key elements in a 10 down machine (5)
8 Failed Allied operation to bypass the Siegfried Line, later immortalized in *Band of Brothers* (6,6)
9 Catastrophic Axis operation to send spies into Britain (4)
11 Name given to MI6 after WWII (inits) (3)
16 Code name for the Allied landing in Provence in August 1944 (7)
17 The central of the five target beaches on 1 across (4)
18 The most heavily defended beach on 1 across (5)

DOWN

1 Official representative of a country (8)
2 Belgian port taken by the Allies in 1944 that later led to the Battle of the Bulge (7)
3 Nazi operation to invade the Soviet Union (10)
4 Major German river that was the focus of Operation 'Plunder' and Operation 'Varsity' (5)
5 Deception campaign, to deflect from Operation 'Overlord' (9)
6 German encryption machine that replaced 10 down for high-level matters in 1940 (6)
10 German encryption system invented in the 1920s by Scherbius (6)
12 Easternmost beach on 1 across (5)
13 German armoured unit (6)
14 Bletchley Park division that cracked 10 down (5)
15 Beach on 1 down between 17 across and 12 down (4)

SOLUTIONS PAGE 215

PUZZLE 111

This sudoku has been encrypted with the letters **AHILMORST**. Solve it to find the word revealed in the shaded boxes.

	O	L	R	T				
		M			A			H
							O	I
	L			R				S
O			I		M			R
R				L			I	
L	R							
A			T			H		
				H	O	R	S	

The next major invasion was the largest amphibious assault of the campaign in April 1945. The target was Okinawa, another outlying island. Operation 'Iceberg' started well, but the US Army and Marine invaders found themselves hampered by difficult terrain and beset by a ferocious Japanese defence that claimed another 12,520 American lives before their objective was achieved.

It was clear that the Japanese would never capitulate, and that an invasion of their mainland would cost many more American lives. So, the United States turned to a new weapon of unparalleled destructive power.

Since 1942, physicist Robert Oppenheimer and the US Army Corps of Engineers had been working on the top-secret Manhattan Project. The results of their research were the first nuclear weapons: a uranium bomb (code name 'Little Boy'); and a plutonium bomb ('Fat Man').

On the morning of 6 August 1945, Colonel Paul W. Tibbets took off in the B-29 Superfortress that he had named after his mother, Enola Gay. His mission was to drop 'Little Boy' on the Japanese city of Hiroshima.

The devastation was unprecedented: a five-mile radius of total destruction and some 100,000 Japanese killed, most of them civilians. Half of the deaths were instantaneous, but others occurred over the following weeks from horrific burns and radiation sickness.

President Truman's appeal for the Japanese to surrender was ignored. So, three days later, 'Fat Man' was dropped on the port of Nagasaki causing even greater horror and carnage. This coincided with a massive Red Army offensive into Japanese-occupied Manchuria.

Japan surrendered on 15 August 1945, bringing the Second World War to an end.

SOLUTIONS PAGE 216

THE COLD WAR

The end of the Second World War changed the global balance of power. Fascism was defeated almost everywhere, with the notable exception of Franco's Spain, but European imperialism was also in decline. The war's two biggest victors raced to fill the vacuum: the ideologically forceful Union of Soviet Socialist Republics (USSR) and the economically powerful United States of America.

A NEW WORLD ORDER

These two superpowers became allies during the war but had mistrusted one another from the outset. The American values of democracy and free market economics were at odds with Soviet communism, and the US had not forgotten that Stalin had originally agreed on a policy of non-aggression with Germany. The Soviets saw the United States as decadent, exploitative and fickle; and they bore a grudge for President Woodrow Wilson's decision to intervene in the Russian Civil War in 1918.

In 1945, as the Second World War drew to a close, Stalin used the presence of Soviet military forces in various countries – such as Hungary, Romania, Bulgaria, Poland and Czechoslovakia – to ensure that declared socialist or communist parties came to power in those nations, giving the West an unnerving glimpse of what they might expect from the USSR in the post-war world. At the Yalta Conference in February, Stalin offhandedly assured the Allies that Soviet-occupied countries would be free and democratic.

US President Franklin D. Roosevelt died in April, just

four months before the end of the Second World War. He was succeeded by Harry S. Truman, who joined Churchill – followed by his successor Clement Attlee – and Stalin at the Potsdam Conference in July to decide how Europe might be administrated and peace maintained. Stalin had already laid claim to much of Central and Eastern Europe, the Baltic states and Poland. At the conference it was agreed that Germany should be split into four occupied zones overseen by Britain, France, the USA and the USSR. Berlin, too, was split into four occupied zones even though it was situated inside the Soviet-controlled area.

PUZZLE 112

Can you divide the grid below into four regions of the same size and shape that each contain one of each of the four flags?

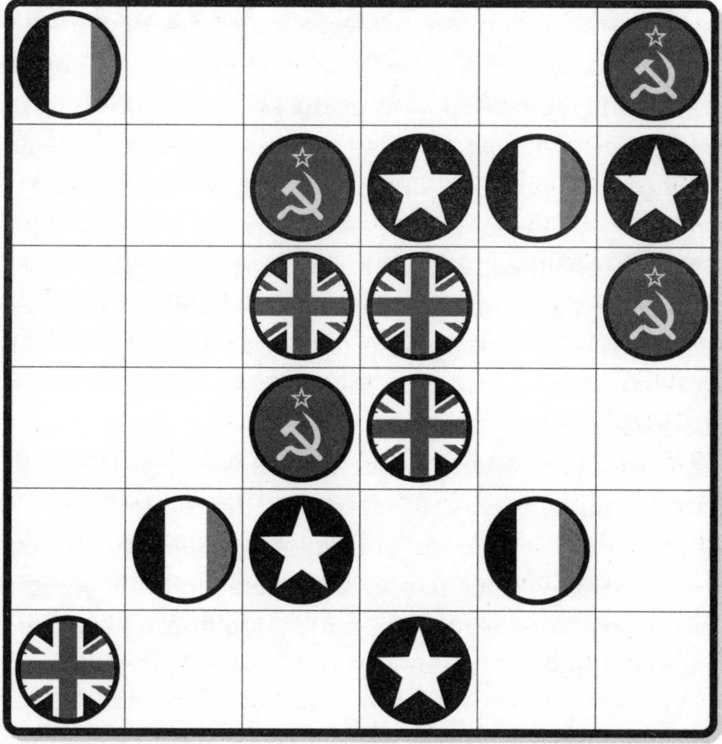

SOLUTIONS PAGE 216

Concerned by Stalin's greed, Truman declared that the US now possessed a game-changing weapon of mass destruction. Stalin's apparent lack of concern was perplexing – Truman did not realize that Soviet spies had already told their leader about the Manhattan Project.

It was only after the Potsdam Conference that the full horror of the atom bomb was unleashed on the people of Hiroshima and Nagasaki in Japan. The Soviet Union began successfully testing its own atomic weapons four years later.

The rumblings of another international conflict caused unease among the battle-fatigued nations. As a result, after the Second World War the largely ineffective League of Nations was replaced by the United Nations, whose remit was more or less the same except it now used force to keep the peace.

Ever distrustful of Stalin, President Truman made the containment of communism the official US foreign policy. The Truman Doctrine was put to the test almost immediately after it was issued in March 1947. The British announced they could no longer provide military support against the communists in the ongoing Greek civil war, allowing the communists to become strong enough to proclaim a provisional government in the north of the country by the end of the year. Although Moscow denied any direct involvement, it had already reneged on a promise to pull out of Iran. Truman reasoned that if Greece turned communist, the Soviets could destabilize neighbouring Turkey, giving them a monopoly in the Mediterranean and oil-rich Middle East.

With millions of dollars of American support, the Greek government forces eventually overthrew the communists. This proxy war would set a precedent for what would become known as the Cold War, with the two superpowers providing military support from afar rather than becoming too directly involved in the actual fighting.

PUZZLE 113

Each letter of the alphabet has been encrypted to a number (1 to 26). Crack the code to solve the puzzle and reveal the Western policy hidden within. To start you off, the codes for three letters have been given.

A		18		1		24		15		12		24		N
B	23 M	26	9	26	23	19		5	22	26	24	20	24	O
C		9		11		12		3		9		26		P
D	5	11	4	24		19	25	25	26	14	5	9	20	Q
E		14				13		19		26		18		R
F	25	4	9	20	19	26	9	23	5	9	20			S
G		23		4						11		18		T
H			24	16	8 P	5	13	10	26	24	26	9	11	U
I		23		13		14		26				4		V
J	25	26	10	26	7	26	17	5		6	16	3	24	W
K		11		24		20		15		4		3		X
L	11	6	5	20	20	4		5	21	16	19	7 L	24	Y
M		20		24		13		14		13		2		Z

1	2	3	4	5	6	7	8	9	10	11	12	13
						L	P					
14	**15**	**16**	**17**	**18**	**19**	**20**	**21**	**22**	**23**	**24**	**25**	**26**
									M			

SOLUTIONS PAGE 217

THE MARSHALL PLAN & NATO

It was clear that containing communism would require spending a lot of money. Fortunately, this was the United States' forte. In 1948, US Secretary of State George C. Marshall initiated a multi-billion dollar package to help Europe recover from the ravages of the Second World War, known as the Marshall Plan. The USSR, who was not a beneficiary of the Marshall Plan, understandably saw the project as a means for the US to buy the loyalty of European nations. Stalin ordered all communist satellites to reject any Marshall Plan aid, blocked Czechoslovakia from joining, and successfully kept the Eastern Bloc in line.

The partitioning of Germany was particularly problematic because, as previously mentioned, its capital Berlin lay within the Soviet-controlled sector. In 1948, Stalin expressed his annoyance at both the Marshall Plan and a decision to change the currency in the French, American and British occupation zones, uniting them economically under the Deutschmark, by blockading the city to prevent supplies from getting in. The Western Allies responded with Operation 'Vittles', which kept the city supplied by a series of airlifts. The following year, the Western Allies combined their occupied zones into the Federal Republic of Germany (West Germany). The Soviets responded by officially designating their zone the German Democratic Republic (East Germany).

In 1949, twelve North American and European countries founded the North Atlantic Treaty Organization (NATO); the Soviets would create their own defensive alliance, the Warsaw Pact, in 1955.

PUZZLE 114

Decrypt this quote. Who said it, and when?

MX QYWX FI XLI TSPMGC SJ XLI YRMXIH WXEXIW XS WYTTSVX JVII TISTPIW ALS EVI VIWMWXMRK EXXIQTXIH WYFNYKEXMSR FC EVQIH QMRSVMXMIW SV FC SYXWMHI TVIWWYVIW

CLUE (Atbash): RMWVKVMWVMXV WZB

PUZZLE 115

Place a mine into some of the empty cells so that each number represents the total count of mines in neighbouring cells, including diagonally adjacent cells.

	2				3			1	2	
2		2		4		4				4
					3					
1		2	4	4				3		4
	1				2		2		4	
1		2		4		2				
			3		3	4		4		
				3					3	2
	4		2		3		2		3	
2			2			1		3		4
		3					1			

SOLUTIONS PAGE 217-8

TAKING SIDES (PART III)

The ideologies and aspirations of the United States and the Soviet Union were incompatible. To understand their motivations, a recap of the events of the previous world wars is needed.

THE SOVIET UNION

In 1917, a Bolshevik revolution in Russia started a civil war which led to the creation of the Union of Soviet Socialist Republics (USSR) in 1922. The revolution's ideology was based on the writings of German philosopher Karl Marx, as interpreted by Bolshevik leader Vladimir Lenin. Marxist-Leninist ideology proposed a classless society where everything was owned by the workers but directed by the ruling Party. Democracy and liberalism were violently suppressed for the good of the people.

Having just pulled Russia out of the 'Great War' with a humiliating concession of territory to Germany, Lenin was not yet in a position to expand his utopia. But he believed his revolution would inspire workers around the world to rise up against their capitalist masters.

After Lenin's death in 1924, the Party eventually came under the control of Joseph Stalin, who might charitably be described as a 'paranoid control freak'. Stalin set his secret police, the NKVD, to work. They rooted out dissent and had everyone Stalin disliked put to death or imprisoned in brutal work camps known as gulags.

Stalin's economic reforms were as impressive as his methods were draconian. His 'Five-Year Plans' massively improved the Soviet Union's production, dragging it into the industrialized twentieth century, albeit at massive and tragic human cost. Unfortunately, much of this work was undone by the Nazi invasion of Russia in 1941. However, despite purging his military of most of its best officers, Stalin's Red Army was able to repel the invaders and expand the Soviet Union's borders – and communist ideology – into Eastern Europe.

THE UNITED STATES

Before the Second World War, the United States was still recovering from the Great Depression. Its entry into the conflict saw a reduction in unemployment, an increase in wages and unprecedented economic growth. When the war ended, it emerged as among the wealthiest nations in the world.

Capitalism, as epitomized by the United States, has links to the Enlightenment and Judeo-Christian morality, with a past marred by slavery and colonialism. Proponents might argue that it is an economic system rather than an ideology. But the inclusion of the words 'In God We Trust' on US currency hint that it could be both, particularly when challenged by a rival system, such as communism. Some of the regimes historically supported by the US were oppressive – for example, some of the Latin American dictatorships or military regimes of the 1960s and 1970s – but they each shared a love of money and a hatred of left-wing political ideas.

United States' foreign policy was influenced by the domino theory that suggested if one nation became communist, its neighbours would follow. Although vocally opposed to imperialism, the US had no misgivings about installing puppet rulers who would suppress any hint of socialism among their people.

PUZZLE 116

Decrypt this quote. Who said it, and when?

AQLJ STOTTDK DK TCO IRHTDN TL TQDOSTO DK TCO RGQDRTDN RK DQLK NUQTRDK CRS GOSNOKGOG RNQLSS TCO NLKTDKOKT

CLUE (Atbash): QLSMKZFOTVLITV

SOLUTIONS PAGE 218

LATIN AMERICA

Some of the United States' southern neighbours were economically poor because their pro-American leaders had made themselves (and the US) wealthier at the people's expense. Without the democratic means to change their situation, the oppressed turned to revolutionary ideologies. The Soviet Union was often happy to lend its support.

In Cuba, military dictator Fulgencio Batista allowed both American companies and organized crime to exploit his country. A cycle of public unrest and draconian rule led to a 1953 revolution engineered by brothers Fidel and Raúl Castro, and Ernesto 'Che' Guevara, that eventually led to his downfall more than five years later.

From 1959 onwards, Castro introduced many socialist reforms. The United States was furious. It financed, trained and organized a counter-assault of Cuban exiles on Cuba's Bay of Pigs in 1961. But the attempt to oust Castro failed and the US changed tactics to concentrate on a trade embargo. This cemented an alliance between Cuba and the Soviet Union that lasted throughout the Cold War and became a major point of tension.

Despite its professed love for democracy, the United States would not permit socialist leaders to prevail, even if they were fairly voted into office. When Salvador Allende was elected president of Chile in 1970, the US plotted a coup which ultimately saw him replaced by the brutal right-wing dictator Augusto Pinochet by 1973.

Even more moderate centre-left governments, who were not communist in nature, were not safe from America's ire. In 1964, Brazil's president, João Goulart, was overthrown by a US-backed coup.

Nicaragua's dynastic dictatorship, the Somoza family, had been installed by the United States in 1936. A successful uprising by the left-wing Sandinista National Liberation Front ended their autocracy and replaced it with a revolutionary government called the Junta of National Reconstruction. In 1981, US-backed insurgents known as the Contras attempted to disrupt and challenge the new government with a guerilla campaign, but were unable to overthrow the Sandinistas. The success of the Sandinistas was punished by US economic sanctions and the country was crippled.

The United States' war on socialist countries in the Caribbean escalated under Ronald Reagan. Reagan's administration supported anti-communist death squads in El Salvador, funded the Contras by selling arms to Iran and even ordered a full-blown invasion of Grenada.

For Latin America, the Cold War's cost in human lives and suffering was catastrophic.

PUZZLE 117

This sudoku has been encrypted with the letters **ABFGIOPSY**. Solve it to find the word revealed in the shaded boxes.

		I	G		A	Y		
		G					O	I
F	P							
A				B				
			S			A	Y	B
Y								O
P				G		I		
	F			P				
	B			I	O			S

SOLUTIONS PAGE 219

AFRICA AND INDIA

During the nineteenth century, European powers colonized much of Africa and southern Asia for their natural resources. After the Second World War, many of these colonies clamoured for independence.

Decolonization was sometimes achieved peacefully, sometimes through armed struggle, and led to the creation of almost one hundred countries whose social and economic stability varied widely. Often countries were partitioned arbitrarily and assigned to different ethnic or religious groups, resulting in resentment and hostility.

Countries of the Cold War world were divided into three economic classifications: the First World, which included the United States and its allies; the Second World, which consisted of China, the Soviet Union and its satellite states; and the Third World, most of which was economically deprived.

The United States supported the self-determination of former colonies but had concerns that poorer nations would succumb to the influence of the Soviet Union. Both superpowers vied for the loyalty of governments with aid and political interference. In 1955, a number of nations, tired of being pawns in the Cold War, joined what would become the Non-Aligned Movement, an organization dedicated to representing the interests and aspirations of developing countries.

A typically tragic example of Cold War decolonization was the Republic of Congo. The country became independent from Belgium in 1960, resulting in a series of civil wars. The Belgians continued to interfere, and Prime Minister Patrice Lumumba asked for help from the US and the UN. The US refused and, while the UN helped, they did not have the mandate for a military intervention. Instead, Lumumba turned to the Soviet Union, but he was overthrown by the Congolese army and murdered by his political opponents. After a series of weak, short-lived attempts at a government, the US gave their financial backing to Joseph Mobutu. They believed he could defend the country against leftist ideas, and Mobutu ruled as a dictator for the next 32 years.

In 1947, the British granted independence to India and split it into two regions: Muslim-majority Pakistan and Hindu-majority India. The new countries developed a bitter rivalry which escalated into armed hostility in 1965. Both expected aid from Britain and the US, but when this was not forthcoming Pakistan developed closer ties to

China and India courted the Soviet Union.

A second war between the two countries in 1971 saw the US take the side of Pakistan and the Soviet Union continue its support for India. However, neither superpower took an active role as they were more concerned with limiting the fallout and negating one another's influence in the region. India was ultimately triumphant and East Pakistan became a separate country, Bangladesh, as a result.

PUZZLE 118

Each letter of the alphabet has been encrypted to a number (1 to 26). Crack the code to solve the puzzle and reveal the Cold War combatants hidden within.

A	■	2	24	11	26	26	4	11	■	7	25	20	26	N
B	10	■	8	■	6	■	10	■	■	■	14	■	6	O
C	3	1	4	10	20	4	5 R	■	20	10	20	4	5	P
D	18	■	4	■	4	■	8	■	10	■	10	■	17	Q
E	6	14	15	4	5	■	25	7	5	6	26	1	■	R
F	25	■	■	■	20	■	16 G	■	19	■	26	■	10	S
G	19	11	3	2	2	7	■	6	7	26	4	4	7	T
H	26	■	10	■	8	■	5	■	4	■	■	■	21	U
I	■	17	5	4	4	9	4	■	5	10	15	15	25	V
J	10	■	10	■	5	■	22	■	26	■	25	■	4	W
K	8	10	13	4	26	■	4	21	1	25	15	25	19	X
L	10	■	10	■	■	■	3	■	25	■	23	■	11	Y
M	11	10	7	12	■	26	19	2 O	20	20	4	24	■	Z

1	2	3	4	5	6	7	8	9	10	11	12	13
	O			R								
14	**15**	**16**	**17**	**18**	**19**	**20**	**21**	**22**	**23**	**24**	**25**	**26**
		G										

SOLUTIONS PAGE 219

ASIA

The newly formed People's Republic of China initially aligned itself with the USSR since the two shared a similar revolutionary Marxist ideology. But relations soured in the 1960s, and China would serve as a counter-balancing force to Soviet influence in Asia.

For the United States, the Cold War would be at its hottest in South East Asia.

Korea had been occupied by Japan during the Second World War and its post-war administration was split between the Soviet Union in the North and the United States in the South. Both trustees set about modelling their Korea in their own ideological image and put the respective nations in the hands of hard-line dictators.

In 1950, the Democratic People's Republic of Korea (North Korea) invaded the Republic of Korea (South Korea). The United States launched a military response but insisted on doing so under the aegis of a United Nations police action. The UN was successful in pushing the North Koreans back across the 38th Parallel and decided to take the opportunity to reunify Korea under a non-communist regime. This looked to be successful until the neighbouring People's Republic of China, concerned that a rival power would soon be at its borders, sent 300,000 troops to help the North.

The Americans and South Koreans were eventually pushed back to the demilitarized zone around the 38th Parallel. The Korean War (1950–53) resulted in a stalemate that caused hundreds of thousands of troops and millions of civilians to be killed and wounded.

In 1955, revolutionary leader Ho Chi Minh, who had freed North Vietnam from French occupation, started a war to liberate the South. As he was a committed Marxist-Leninist, this caused alarm in Washington, D.C. and the United States was once again on a war footing, even resorting to conscription to keep communism out of Vietnam.

The ensuing Vietnam War had a vastly different character to the more conventional Korean War. Fought largely in dense jungle, the technologically superior US forces faced both the North Vietnamese Army and the guerrilla troops of the Viet Cong, who were able to take full advantage of their native terrain and blend into the populace at will. American atrocities against the civilian population reinforced the defenders' resolve and brought condemnation of US involvement in the conflict.

The Vietnam War was the first major conflict to be televised. Although initially supported at home, over time the American people felt misled by their government and an anti-war movement gained traction as more and more coffins were brought back from the remote Asian jungle.

After nearly 18 years, at a cost of over 100 billion dollars and around 58,200 American lives, the United States withdrew, having completely underestimated the determination of its enemy.

In 1975, after Vietnam had unified as a communist state, neighbouring Cambodia also became a Marxist regime, although without the blessing of the Soviet Union. The China-backed Khmer Rouge ruled Cambodia as a genocidal dictatorship that massacred approximately a quarter of the country's population.

PUZZLE 119

Can you unscramble the names of eight countries below, which have each had their letters jumbled up and some spaces introduced? One extra letter has also been added to each name which, when all eight are extracted and read in order from top to bottom, will spell out a word relating to their Cold War connection.

1. BUGLE AIM

2. ATTITUDES SENT

3. MIDDLING TO NUKE

4. A POLAR GUT

5. NARY WON

6. ENTRANTS HELD

7. ARMED INK

8. CALCINED

SOLUTIONS PAGE 120

THE MIDDLE EAST

The demise of the Ottoman Empire in the Great War created a patchwork of nations that would never again enjoy prolonged peace or stability. While Turkey turned towards Europe and a more secular society, others adopted Islamic governments with elements of imperialism, Arab nationalism and/or socialism.

Some areas were initially administrated by western imperial powers, who decolonized and partitioned nations, drawing lines on a map with little apparent regard for the consequences.

In 1917, Britain had made a promise (the Balfour Declaration) to create a 'national home for the Jewish people' in Palestine. Jewish immigration to the area increased substantially during the 1920s and 1930s, increasing tensions with the Palestinian Arabs. After the Second World War, relations worsened and the British handed the problem over to the United Nations who partitioned the region and created the nation of Israel, leading to even greater tensions.

Israel declared independence in 1948, which angered its Arab League neighbours and led to a war. The Israelis were victorious and added more territory to their new nation. Another war broke out in 1967 which saw Israel further expand its borders. Predictably, the Cold War superpowers took an interest in this source of perpetual conflict; the United States standing by Israel and the Soviet Union providing aid to its enemies.

British rule in Egypt came to an end in 1952 with a revolution that replaced the country's monarchy with a republic, orchestrated in part by Gamal Abdel Nasser, who later became President of Egypt' A secular reformist, Nasser wanted to keep Egypt neutral in the Cold War while maintaining good relations with both sides. However, the United States was mistrustful of anyone who would not condemn communism and withdrew aid from the country, going back on a promise to fund Egypt's Aswan High Dam project. In response, Nasser ordered the seizure of the Suez Canal, which had belonged to the French and British. With the help of Israel, France and Britain launched an attack to retake the area. Although successful, the action was a diplomatic catastrophe, known as the Suez Crisis. Condemned by both the Soviet Union and the United States, Britain was forced to withdraw from Egypt resulting in an irreparable loss of face.

During the Cold War, many regional conflicts were exacerbated by the interference of the United States and the Soviet Union. However, local differences were temporarily put aside when the Soviets invaded Afghanistan and found themselves facing Mujahideen fighters from rival Sunni and Shia factions supported by American money and CIA training. This costly and ultimately futile adventure became the Soviet Union's Vietnam War. They were not the first or last nation to make this mistake.

Foreign interference aside, the Middle East had a Cold War of its own between Saudi Arabia and Iran.

Saudi Arabia emerged from the ruins of the Ottoman Empire. It became enormously wealthy when oil reserves were discovered in 1938 and it quickly developed ties with the United States. Saudi Arabia is also at the heart of the Islamic world - the holy cities of Mecca and Medina are located within its borders - and the majority of Saudis follow the Sunni branch of Islam.

In 1979, an Islamic Revolution in Iran overthrew its American puppet ruler, the Shah Mohammad Reza Pahlavi. Iran was also a significant oil-producing nation and most of its citizens followed the Shia branch of Islam. This made it Saudi Arabia's main economic and religious rival, as well as a cultural threat, especially if it could export its anti-American, anti-monarchist ideology to other Muslim countries. Proxy wars between Saudi Arabia and Iran have devastated nearby Iraq, Syria, Lebanon, Palestine and Yemen. At the time of writing their Cold War is still ongoing.

EUROPE

In many ways the Cold War was a continuation of the First World War and the Second World War. And the front line was located at the epicentre of those conflicts: Europe.

Stalin's land grab at the end of the Second World War might have been more far-reaching had the Allies not initiated Operation 'Overlord' and raced to liberate much of occupied Western Europe before the Red Army arrived. As it was, Stalin gained control of most of Eastern Europe and a large portion of Germany. One of the first major crises of the Cold War was the Berlin Blockade (1948–49), Stalin's failed attempt to control the capital.

It was hoped that Stalin's death in 1953 might lead to positive reforms. An uprising in East Germany later that year, however, was suppressed by Soviet troops and state police. Under Stalin's successor Nikita Khrushchev, the East German secret police, the Stasi, still maintained a grip on the population. This, understandably, led to many East Germans wanting to move to the liberal West. To stop the flow of refugees, Khrushchev ordered the construction of the Berlin Wall in 1961 – a concrete barrier that came to symbolize the divisions of the Cold War.

To create a stronger sense of unity between the Soviet Union and its satellite states, Khrushchev founded the Warsaw Pact – the Soviet answer to NATO – in 1955. Austria was declared a neutral country and became a preferred location for diplomatic talks between the superpowers. However, Warsaw Pact countries that voiced dissatisfaction with the Soviet regime continued to face harsh penalties. In 1956, an uprising brought down the communist government of Hungary but a new regime was quickly and brutally installed after the Red Army sent its tanks into Budapest.

Western Europe was ideologically relaxed compared to the Eastern Bloc and even the United States. Socialist opposition parties and movements were tolerated, even when they demonstrated anti-establishment sentiments. It was sufficient to remind the population of the West of their prosperity compared to the impoverished citizens of Eastern Europe. Ultimately it was this economic and democratic disparity that would bring down the Soviet project.

PUZZLE 120

Shade the cells so that each number represents the total number of shaded cells touching that cell, including diagonally, and including itself. Is anything revealed?

	4	2				3	4			
5		4			7			3		3
3	5		5	3	6	3	6	3		3
	7		6		7		5		5	
		3			5					
4								3		
	4	3		3	4		2			3
	5		4		6	3	2	4	5	
	3	3			4				3	
			4					3	3	3
	4				4	2				

PUZZLE 121

Can you find five words or names relating to the space race hidden in the sentences below? For example, the word 'star' is hidden in the phrase 'we must arrange a launch'.

1. The control room is silent before a mission commences.
2. The technical director bitterly regretted his team's failures.
3. A poll – or popular vote – will be held to name the new department.
4. With spies, there's always a tell; I tend to spot traitors a mile off.
5. That event will always be seen as a technological miracle.

SOLUTIONS PAGE 220-1

LIFE IN THE COLD WAR

If the two previous global wars had been a military competition, the Cold War was a battle to be *better* – at everything. To prevent the other side's ideology from gaining converts, the superpowers constantly vied for supremacy in fields as diverse as sport and science.

THE ARMS RACE

For many, life during the Cold War was overshadowed by the possibility of an apocalypse. Although the US had expedited the Japanese surrender by dropping atom bombs, which in turn led to the end of the Second World War, it became clear that a war fought exclusively with these weapons would end with no winner.

By 1949, both superpowers had atom bombs. Three years later the United States upped the ante by testing the first hydrogen bomb, which was far more destructive than the bombs dropped on Nagasaki and Hiroshima. Further advances saw bombs replaced by rockets with ever-increasing ranges and payloads, culminating in the intercontinental ballistic missile (ICBM).

In 1954, President Eisenhower – through a speech made by his Secretary of State John Foster Dulles – made it clear to the Soviet Union that if it used its nuclear weapons against the United States or its allies, the US would not hesitate to respond. This understanding was later called Mutually Assured Destruction (MAD) and it maintained an uneasy peace, at least while the nuclear arsenals of both sides were in balance. The problem was that both sides kept building more nuclear weapons, forcing the other to follow suit, and the nuclear arms race was on.

No nation wanted a nuclear war but the constant fear of one was palpable. In the coming decades, both the US and UK televised ultra-realistic dramas such as *The War Game*, *Threads* and *The Day After* which showed the full horror of a nuclear attack and its after-effects on the civilian population. There were also government-produced public information films like 'Protect and Survive' which offered little help or hope but contributed to the climate of despair. A popular meme suggested the leaders of both superpowers had only to press a big red launch button to trigger the end of the world.

Perhaps the closest the world came to doomsday was during the 1962 Cuban Missile Crisis. The failed American invasion of Cuba led Fidel Castro to ask Khrushchev for a local nuclear deterrent. The Soviets complied since they already felt threatened by NATO's medium-range nuclear missiles in Italy and Turkey.

With nuclear launch sites just 140 kilometres from Florida, President John F. Kennedy's military advisors suggested a full-blown attack on Cuba. But JFK's response was ultimately more restrained. He ordered a naval 'quarantine' to prevent more missiles being brought to the islands. However, the Soviets saw the restriction as a blockade, an act of war. Both countries were put on high alert and one of the Soviet submarines came dangerously close to launching a nuclear missile. Fortunately, diplomacy prevailed. Washington withdrew its missiles from Turkey, and Moscow removed its missiles from Cuba.

In 1957, the United Kingdom tested its own H-bomb and became the world's third atomic power. That same year saw the birth of the Campaign for Nuclear Disarmament (CND). This movement to 'ban the bomb' started small but grew substantially over the next two decades. On 12 June 1982 around a million people gathered in New York's Central Park to protest the nuclear arms race.

By the end of the 1960s, the superpowers had started to listen to public dissent. In the Strategic Arms Limitation Treaty (SALT) of 1972 both sides pledged to limit and partially disarm their nuclear arsenals. Further treaties were signed over the coming years, including SALT II and START and the INF that further limited the superpowers' nuclear capabilities.

PUZZLE 122

What do these three men have in common and who is the odd one out?

Clark Kent **Stanislav Petrov** **Vasili Arkhipov**

SOLUTIONS PAGE 221

SPIES

Information was precious in the Cold War and the techniques for obtaining and obfuscating it became more sophisticated.

Joseph Stalin set a paranoid precedent with his constant need to be told of enemies both within and without. From the 1950s, the Soviet Union had two principal intelligence agencies: the MVD (interior secret police) and the KGB, whose remit ranged from state security to foreign intelligence.

The United States' equivalent agencies were the Federal Bureau of Investigation (FBI) and the Central Intelligence Agency (CIA). Under President Truman, the FBI was ordered to seek out subversive individuals and organizations on American soil, and Truman made explicit with his 'Loyalty' programme that all government employees could be investigated for any hints of subversion. In June 1953, Julius Rosenberg, a US Army Signal Corps engineer, and his wife Ethel were executed for spying; they had procured critical information about nuclear weapon design for the Soviet Union.

Not all investigations were based on concrete evidence, however. Fear that communism had infiltrated American society inflamed suspicion of anyone with unconventional ideas. Proponents of these witch-hunts included FBI director J. Edgar Hoover and Wisconsin Senator Joseph McCarthy, who were closely associated with the House inquisition that led to many innocents losing their livelihoods.

William August Fisher not an innocent – British-born but having grown up in Russia, he adopted the name Rudolph Ivanovic Abel and joined the predecessor to the KGB. He was sent to the United States where he posed as an artist and spied for nine years before a fellow agent defected and turned him in.

On 1 May 1960, a forthcoming summit between NATO and the Soviet Union was derailed when an American U2 spy plane was shot down over Russia. President Eisenhower denied accusations of espionage, claiming it was a weather plane that had strayed off course. However, the captured pilot, Francis Gary Powers, was in possession of enough evidence to incriminate him. Khrushchev was furious and stormed out of the summit. Powers was sentenced to ten years for spying, but in 1962 was returned to the United States in a prisoner exchange with Rudolph Ivanovic Abel.

Secret agents engaged the popular imagination, with Ian Fleming's fictional James Bond being the best-known, although his glamorous lifestyle was not realistic. Perhaps the most famous British spies of the period are the Cambridge Five: Anthony Blunt, Guy Burgess, John Cairncross, Donald Maclean and Kim Philby. They successfully passed large amounts of information to the Soviet Union and were a source of embarrassment to British Intelligence and the government.

PUZZLE 123

Each letter of the alphabet has been encrypted to a number (1 to 26). Crack the code to solve the puzzle and reveal the new danger hidden within.

A	5	21	22	26	1	20	■	10	1	5	10	14	17	**N**
B	■	2	■	13	■	14	■	12	■	16	■	2	■	**O**
C	7	21	13 A	24	■	6	2 N	17	6	14	2	1	20	**P**
D	■	3	■	26	■	5	■	16	■	4	■	14	■	**Q**
E	26	21	25	17	8	13	16	6	■	17	14	2	3	**R**
F	■	13	■	■	■	10	■	14	■	20	■	■	■	**S**
G	13	26	25	13	26	1	■	2	14	10	1	11	18	**T**
H	■	■	■	22	■	22	■	21	■	■	■	1	■	**U**
I	10	14	11	21	■	1	2	20	14	6	1	2	9 G	**V**
J	■	16	■	3	■	26	■	26	■	13	■	24	■	**W**
K	6	13	19	1	6	1	15	17	■	26	14	1	2	**X**
L	■	10	■	23	■	10	■	13	■	17	■	2	■	**Y**
M	16	17	6	17	24	18	■	16	17	3	1	9	2	**Z**

1	2	3	4	5	6	7	8	9	10	11	12	13
	N							G				A
14	**15**	**16**	**17**	**18**	**19**	**20**	**21**	**22**	**23**	**24**	**25**	**26**

SOLUTIONS PAGE 222

THE SPACE RACE

A by-product of the nuclear arms race was the creation of the world's first spacecraft. In 1957, the Soviet Union test-launched the first intercontinental ballistic missile, the *R-7 Semyorka.* Designed to carry up to a five-megaton warhead as much as 8,000 kilometres, its existence caused understandable concern in the United States, given the distance between Moscow and Washington, D.C. is only 7,800 kilometres.

Just over a month later the Soviets launched the world's first artificial satellite, *Sputnik 1,* into orbit and caused the Americans even more concern. Somehow the Soviet Union had achieved a technological lead and their satellites would give them an enormous advantage in surveillance. But the Russians were far from finished. In November, they launched *Sputnik 2* which sent the first living thing into space: a dog called Laika.

The following year, the United States founded the National Aeronautics and Space Administration (NASA) and made up some ground in the space race by launching the first communications satellite and the first solar-powered satellite. In August 1959 they took the first photograph of Earth from an orbiting satellite. The Soviets replied with the first photographs of the far side of the Moon.

In the 1960s, the space race became a sprint. On 31 January 1961 the US launched the first hominid into space: a chimpanzee named Ham. But the Soviets managed to get an actual human – Yuri Gagarin – into orbit just over two months later.

America was having some success exploring the solar system with the first probes to Mars and Venus, but the moment that really caught the public's imagination was when President John F. Kennedy vowed that the US would put a man on the Moon by the end of the decade. This was finally accomplished when astronaut Neil Armstrong declared 'That's one small step for a man, one giant leap for mankind' on 20 July 1969.

Although the space race was every bit as earnest as the other Cold War competitions, the exploits of Soviet cosmonauts and American astronauts held public attention on both sides of the Iron Curtain. In July 1975, a joint Apollo-Soyuz mission saw spacecraft from both sides dock together and the crew shake hands – a powerful symbol of cooperation that brought the space race to an amicable end.

PUZZLE 124

This sudoku has been encrypted with the letters **ACEILMNST**. Solve it to find the word revealed in the shaded boxes.

	I			L				
		N	M		A			
					I	N		C
N		T		M			C	
C								N
	M			E		T		S
L		S	T					
			I		L	A		
				S			L	

SOLUTIONS PAGE 222

THE COLD WAR ENDS

The Soviet Union was founded on a repressive version of Marxism that could increase production (if not happiness) but never on the scale of American consumer capitalism. Under Stalin, it had been a cult of personality built around a leader none dared question. After his death, his successor, Nikita Khrushchev, attempted to bring about reform with 'de-Stalinization', but the state remained a single-party autocracy with a deep mistrust of the West.

By the end of the 1960s, the West had enjoyed an economic boom, but that did not mean there was unanimous satisfaction. Workers demanded better conditions and wages, women continued their struggle for social and economic parity and minorities spoke out against discrimination. A growing awareness of the detrimental effects of Western interference in poorer countries sparked protests, particularly among students. None of these issues were completely fixed but, on the whole, activism led to reform.

On the other side of the Iron Curtain, people were also demanding change, but reform came slowly and, in countries like Czechoslovakia and Hungary, it was suppressed with harsh reprisals. The 1970s saw upheavals on both sides, with government corruption exposed and proxy wars draining the public coffers and goodwill. After an economically stagnant decade, the West saw the election of free-market governments in the US (Ronald Reagan), the UK (Margaret Thatcher) and West Germany (Helmut Kohl).

A diversity of anti-communist sentiment swept through Eastern Europe in the 1980s, from nationalist movements and Western-inspired punk rock to the Catholic Church. In Poland, the trade union Solidarity, with the support of the United States, the Vatican and ten million members rose up against the Soviet-backed regime.

By 1985, when premier Mikhail Gorbachev came to power, the United States had a comfortable lead in an arms race that had crippled the Soviet economy. Gorbachev was still committed to socialist ideals but proposed two radical reforms. The first was *glasnost* ('openness'), which brought an end to the censorship and secrecy that had been a trademark of the communist regime. The other was *perestroika* – a restructuring of the Soviet Union's economy making it freer, more competitive and more efficient.

However, once the floodgates of freedom opened, the old order was swept away. One by one the satellite nations that had composed the USSR declared their independence. On 9 November 1989, the Berlin Wall fell and at the Malta Summit three weeks later the United States and Soviet Union declared an end to the Cold War.

On 25 December 1991, after 69 years, the Soviet Union came to an end.

PUZZLE 125

Each letter of the alphabet has been encrypted to a number (1 to 26). Crack the code to solve the puzzle and reveal the dangerous game hidden within. To start you off, the codes for three letters have been given.

A	21	26	17	12	2	■	12	18	25	10	7	21 S	6	N
B	■	6	■	22	■	12	■	17	■	20	■	24	■	O
C	16	25	11	22	20	14	14 T	7	■	13	12	23	10	P
D	■	14	■	12	■	14	■	11	■	13	■	20	■	Q
E	17	25	18	18	20	17	■	19	11	12	8	20	■	R
F	■	■	■	10	■	7	■	13	■	■	■	3	■	S
G	17	20	10	2	■	18	12	12	■	18	2	20	21	T
H	■	15	■	■	■	23	■	11	■	17	■	■	■	U
I	■	20	1	12	10	14	■	21	14	25	17	13	21	V
J	■	16	■	26	■	12	■	6	■	12	■	12	■	W
K	12	14	25	26	■	18	23	7	10	9	7	11	4	X
L	■	20	■	10	■	10	■	26	■	20	■	4	■	Y
M	12	9 D	6	20	17	20	21	■	12	17	17	25	5	Z

1	2	3	4	5	6	7	8	9	10	11	12	13
								D				
14	**15**	**16**	**17**	**18**	**19**	**20**	**21**	**22**	**23**	**24**	**25**	**26**
T							S					

SOLUTIONS PAGE 223

PUZZLE 126

Can you complete this Cold War-themed crossword? If you are struggling with some of the answers, reading the rest of this chapter might help.

ACROSS

3 Nuclear missiles located there led to a crisis with the US (4)
5 Canal that was the cause of an Egyptian invasion (4)
7 Group of countries; the Soviet ___ (4)
8 US Moon-landing programme (6)
9 First Soviet satellite in space (7)
11 2 down, for example (8)
16 The Soviet Union, for short (inits) (4)
17 First Russian – and first man – in space, Gagarin (4)
18 Economic association of East European countries founded in 1949 (7)
19 Name of the first animal to go into 14 down (5)

DOWN

1 System of government for countries in 2 down (9)
2 International organization formed in 1949 by Western countries (inits) (4)
4 Devastatingly effective form of modern weapon (6)
5 Soviet leader until 1953 (6)
6 Violent seizure of power from a government (4)
10 Formal international agreement (6)
12 Fire a missile, perhaps (6)
13 Collection of weapons (7)
14 Curved path taken around a body in space (5)
15 16 across, in Russia (inits) (4)

PUZZLE 127

In the word search grid are the first names and surnames of the nine US Presidents who held office during the Cold War. They may appear horizontally, vertically or diagonally, backwards or forwards. Can you find them all and match them with their descriptions?

A	D	M	J	W	N	Z	B	D	O	T	N	C	D	W
X	E	S	G	A	V	G	B	H	R	A	J	W	B	L
R	X	B	M	E	U	U	Y	Y	G	A	I	U	L	P
A	V	U	R	I	O	L	V	A	R	G	H	Y	P	N
R	R	S	O	S	V	R	E	H	H	R	N	C	B	B
T	U	H	N	E	M	R	G	T	F	D	A	T	I	Z
T	L	P	A	N	Q	E	V	E	O	Y	P	H	B	R
Z	T	H	L	H	N	T	P	N	R	C	G	G	C	V
V	W	J	D	O	O	R	H	Z	D	M	V	R	D	P
P	B	A	L	W	X	A	N	O	S	N	H	O	J	E
V	G	G	A	E	I	C	G	T	L	E	Y	C	J	B
P	J	A	R	R	N	U	U	F	A	T	M	O	P	N
W	J	O	E	M	B	N	G	L	B	M	H	A	N	F
L	Z	B	G	Y	I	Y	D	E	N	N	E	K	J	L
X	B	O	S	S	P	D	W	B	J	X	Q	P	Q	P

1. Devised the policy of 'Containment', as well as the Marshall Plan and the creation of NATO. Led the US/UN police action in the Korean War.

2. Became the first Supreme Allied Commander Europe (NATO). Devised the policy of 'Massive Retaliation' in the event of a nuclear attack. Authorized the establishment of NASA.

3. The first US president born in the twentieth century. A strong advocate for both the nuclear arms race and the space race. Approved the failed Bay of Pigs invasion against Cuba. Assassinated in Dallas, Texas.

4. Committed over half a million troops to the Vietnam War. Started the policy known as 'détente' to ease tensions between the US and Soviet Union.

5. Ended US involvement in the Vietnam War. First president to visit communist China. Resigned from office following a political scandal.

6. Following his predecessor's resignation, became the first president to take office without being voted in by the Electoral College. Signed the Helsinki Accords to improve détente with the Soviet Union.

7. Former peanut farmer. Pardoned Vietnam War draft evaders. Ended détente when the Soviet Union invaded Afghanistan.

8. Former Hollywood actor. Labelled the Soviet Union an 'Evil Empire'. Became embroiled in the Iran-Contra affair of which he denied any knowledge. Ordered the invasion of Grenada.

9. Famously promised 'Read my lips: no new taxes', which he reneged on when he took office. Signed the Strategic Arms Reduction Treaty (START).

SOLUTIONS PAGE 223-4

SOLUTIONS

PUZZLE 1

The number '1'. Hold the puzzle up to a mirror and the answer becomes clear. 'Contemplate' is a synonym of 'reflect'.

PUZZLE 2

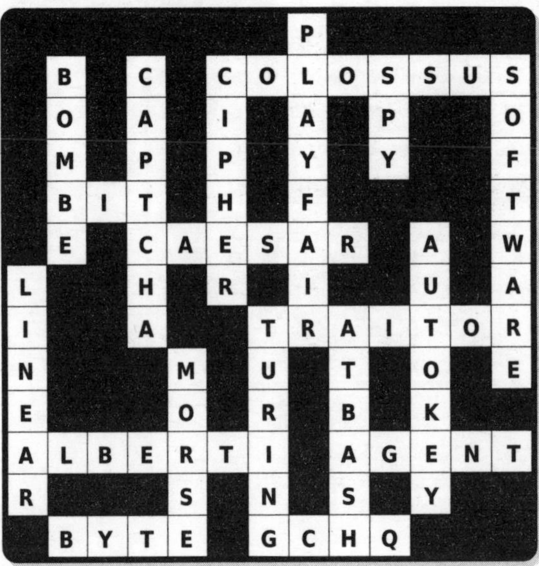

PUZZLE 3

The rather clumsily embedded name of a London railway station is a clue. From that you can discern that every fourth word of the text is the real message.

The afternoon was ***hot*** *but those mad* ***dogs****, all sweaty and* ***tanned****, were still loitering* ***outside****. They preened like* ***kings*** *while I grew* ***cross*** *and quite exasperated.* ***Oh****, it would be* ***nigh*** *on impossible to* ***know*** *what they came* ***for****.*

Hot dog stand outside Kings Cross 09.04

PUZZLE 4

The hidden word was **STEGANOGRAPHY.**

A	D	R	E	W		O	B	J	E	C	T	E	D	N
B		E		E		B		U		O		V		O
C	E	Q	U	A	T	E		M	A	Y	H	E	M	P
D		U		R		Y		P		P				Q
E	S	E	M	I		S	T	I	M	U	L	U	S	R
F		S		N				N				N		S
G	S	T	E	G	A	N	O	G	R	A	P	H	Y	T
H		E				E				P		E		U
I	A	D	V	O	C	A	T	E		O	I	L	Y	V
J				Z		R		S		L		P		W
K	E	N	R	O	B	E		S	C	O	F	F	S	X
L		I		N		S		A		G		U		Y
M	E	X	P	E	R	T	L	Y		Y	O	L	K	Z

1	2	3	4	5	6	7	8	9	10	11	12	13
O	B	I	L	K	Q	C	W	H	F	Y	P	E
14	**15**	**16**	**17**	**18**	**19**	**20**	**21**	**22**	**23**	**24**	**25**	**26**
N	Z	M	T	A	V	J	G	S	X	R	D	U

PUZZLE 5

'D' for December.

• — — —	July
• —	August
• • •	September
— — —	October
— •	November
— • •	**DECEMBER**
• — — —	January
• • — •	February
— —	March
• —	April
— —	May
• — — —	June

PUZZLE 6

●	2	●	●	1		1
	3	4	4		3	●
2	●		●	●	4	●
3	●	4	3		3	●
●			●	2		2
2		2		●	3	●
●	2	●		●		

PUZZLE 7

Frank handed the bartender three quarters, a dime and three nickels, making one dollar. If he had wanted Lite, he would have kept the dime in his pocket.

PUZZLE 8

I	G	B	H	F	J	F	K	E	N	R	R	H	G	G
T	Q	T	Y	O	A	I	N	N	N	A	F	Y	S	O
R	J	K	M	K	D	C	K	F	O	B	K	H	S	Q
E	W	C	O	J	R	A	Z	N	I	Y	S	P	I	X
B	M	G	K	Y	F	T	B	O	T	A	F	A	S	J
L	E	T	P	K	S	B	P	I	I	L	C	R	Y	B
A	S	T	R	V	E	A	E	T	S	P	E	G	L	P
V	S	B	F	D	T	S	K	U	O	H	G	O	A	X
V	A	W	M	L	R	H	A	T	P	A	R	N	N	X
T	G	H	E	O	L	C	Y	I	S	B	U	A	A	S
P	E	D	M	C	E	U	C	T	N	E	D	G	P	H
E	O	M	D	C	K	B	N	S	A	T	V	E	K	I
C	C	K	S	M	K	U	Q	B	R	W	Q	T	W	F
P	D	S	R	B	K	E	V	U	T	N	O	S	S	T
Z	H	E	N	A	W	J	Y	S	M	R	D	W	C	O

ALBERTI
ALPHABET
ANALYSIS
ATBASH
CIPHER
CODE
ENCRYPT
KEY
MESSAGE
MORSE
NULL
SHIFT
STEGANOGRAPHY
SUBSTITUTION
TRANSPOSITION

PUZZLE 9

DIT!

M	▬ ▬	Mercury
V	• • • ▬	Venus
E	•	**EARTH**
M	▬ ▬	Mars
J	• ▬ ▬ ▬	Jupiter
S	• • •	Saturn
U	• • ▬	Uranus
N	▬ •	Neptune

PUZZLE 10

D	S	E	C	O
O	E	D	S	C
S	O	C	E	D
C	D	S	O	E
E	C	O	D	S

PUZZLE 11

The hidden word was **CRYPTOLOGY.**

A	■	■	S	■	M	■	E	■	G	■	S	■	■	N
B	L	I	P	P	Y	■	D	R	O	O	P	Y	■	O
C	E	■	E	■	T	■	I	■	O	■	A	■	C	P
D	G	R	A	P	H	I	C	■	D	I	N	A	R	Q
E	I	■	K	■	S	■	T	■	B	■	■	■	Y	R
F	T	R	E	K	■	D	■	H	Y	S	S	O	P	S
G	I	■	R	■	P	I	X	I	E	■	E	■	T	T
H	M	O	S	Q	U	E	■	C	■	E	R	G	O	U
I	A	■	■	■	Z	■	S	■	F	■	V	■	L	V
J	T	O	P	A	Z	■	T	O	R	N	A	D	O	W
K	E	■	U	■	L	■	A	■	O	■	N	■	G	X
L	■	I	N	J	E	C	T	■	W	I	T	T	Y	Y
M	■	■	T	■	D	■	E	■	N	■	S	■	■	Z

1	2	3	4	5	6	7	8	9	10	11	12	13
P	U	Y	Q	B	X	F	T	L	G	R	C	M
14	**15**	**16**	**17**	**18**	**19**	**20**	**21**	**22**	**23**	**24**	**25**	**26**
J	S	O	K	W	H	V	I	A	N	D	E	Z

PUZZLE 12

WELL THANKS FOR NOTHING

W				T				K				R				H			
	E		L		H		N		S		O		N		T		I		G
		L				A				F				O				N	

PUZZLE 13

The keyword is **DEVIL.**

The message reads:
CAN YOU PICK UP THE KIDS FROM SCHOOL

D	E	I	L	V
C	A	Y	O	N
U	P	C	K	I
U	P	H	E	T
K	I	S	F	D
R	O	S	C	M
H	O	L	X	O

PUZZLE 14

א1
ת2
ב3
ש4

PUZZLE 15

The abridged wisdom of Benjamin Franklin was first encrypted with Atbash and then put through the rail fence.

G				V				P				Z				I				U				Z				V		
	S		V		X		M		V		K		H		X		V		R		G		L		I		W		Z	
		I				Z				V				V				G				D				V				W

GSIVVXZMPVVKZHVXIVGRUGDLZIVWVZW
three can keep a secret if two are dead

PUZZLE 16

'I came, I saw, I conquered.'

Coined by Julius Caesar. V is the Roman numeral for 5, which is the number of shifts required to crack the code using the Caesar shift cipher.

PUZZLE 17

Each word is a letter from the International Code of Signals. Putting them in order gives you the ANSWER.

3. ALPHA
5. NOVEMBER
4. SIERRA
1. WHISKEY
2. ECHO
6. ROMEO

PUZZLE 18

Veni Vidi Vici. The original quote from Julius Caesar, using his preferred three-shift key.

PUZZLE 19

The sequence is the number of letters in the words for 1 to 12.

ONE	3
TWO	3
THREE	5
FOUR	4
FIVE	4
SIX	**3**
SEVEN	5
EIGHT	5
NINE	4
TEN	3
ELEVEN	6
TWELVE	6

PUZZLE 20

The picture reveals ATBASH, but further encoded in Atbash itself.

PUZZLE 21

James Winston, Winston Lee and Lee James.

PUZZLE 22

Clue: *mahatma bapu* ('great soul' and 'father' were names given to Mohandas Karamchand Gandhi).

Keyword: GANDHI

Message: *'Be the change that you wish to see in the world.'*

PUZZLE 23

The text is from the United States Declaration of Independence and was encrypted with the Caesar shift cipher (4 shifts):

We hold these truths to be self-evident, that all men are created equal, that they are endowed by their creator with certain unalienable rights, that among these are life, liberty and the pursuit of happiness. That to secure these rights, governments are instituted among men, deriving their just powers from the consent of the governed – that whenever any form of government becomes destructive of these ends, it is the right of the people to alter or to abolish it, and to institute new government, laying its foundation on such principles and organizing its powers in such form, as to them shall seem most likely to effect their safety and happiness.

PUZZLE 24

1. Fill the jug to capacity, so the jug contains five pints.
2. Pour the water from the jug to fill the jar, so the jug has two pints and the jar has three pints.
3. Empty the jar.
4. Pour the contents of the jug into the jar, so the jar contains two pints.
5. Fill the jug to capacity
6. Pour the water from the jug into the jar until the jar is full, so the jug now has four pints and the jar has three pints.
7. Empty the jar and take the jug home.

PUZZLE 25

The key was an anagram and can be rearranged as: **LISTEN**.

The plaintext is a quote from Elizabeth I:

'Do not tell secrets to those whose faith and silence you have not already tested.'

PUZZLE 26

ITHINKIMINLOVEWITHYOU.

Your ally clearly has great taste and no subtlety!

PUZZLE 27

1. **Atbash:** The diplomat bashfully admitted to copying confidential documents.
2. **Morse:** Start by checking whether it's an anagram, or see if there are any letters missing.
3. **Pigpen:** For the first mission, he was the perfect guinea pig; pensive, hard-working and suspicious of everyone.
4. **Shift:** We can't afford to be slapdash if there's an issue of national security at stake.
5. **Autokey:** You'll need to use intelligence from the Bureau to key in the right codes.

PUZZLE 28

P	X	I	A	D	L	T	E	N
E	L	D	X	T	N	I	A	P
T	N	A	P	I	E	D	L	X
D	T	L	I	X	P	A	N	E
I	E	P	D	N	A	X	T	L
X	A	N	L	E	T	P	I	D
A	P	T	N	L	X	E	D	I
N	D	E	T	P	I	L	X	A
L	I	X	E	A	D	N	P	T

PUZZLE 29

Four cigarettes. He can create three from the cigarettes he has collected, and one more from the residue of the three he constructed.

PUZZLE 30

B. Each box contains two letters in Morse code. If you work out the Caesar shift between the two letters, you find that each row and each column contains a box of shift 1, 2, 3 and 4. The missing box is shift 4 (O and S).

1 BC	2 RT	3 EH	4 KO
4 IM	3 TW	2 IK	1 ST
3 FI	4 OS	1 RS	2 EG
2 VX	1 AB	4 HL	3 OR

PUZZLE 31

The word is **ENIGMATIC**.

F	E	H	C	G	D	B	I	A
A	D	C	F	I	B	H	G	E
B	G	I	E	H	A	F	C	D
I	C	B	A	F	E	G	D	H
G	A	F	H	D	I	E	B	C
E	H	D	B	C	G	I	A	F
H	F	G	I	A	C	D	E	B
C	I	E	D	B	F	A	H	G
D	B	A	G	E	H	C	F	I

0	7	1	2	6	3	5	8	4
3	6	5	7	8	4	1	2	0
2	4	8	1	5	0	6	3	7
6	1	4	0	3	5	8	7	2
8	2	3	6	1	7	0	4	5
5	0	7	8	4	2	3	1	6
1	5	6	4	2	8	7	0	3
4	8	0	3	7	6	2	5	1
7	3	2	5	0	1	4	6	8

B	H	A	F	G	F	I	D	A
+3	+1	+0	+8	+13	+7	+0	+3	+2
E	I	A	N	T	M	I	G	C

PUZZLE 32

PUZZLE 33

Franz simply takes the hat from his head, places it over the barrel of his gun and fires!

PUZZLE 34

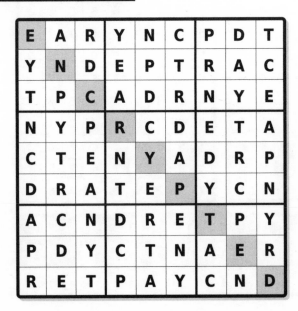

E	A	R	Y	N	C	P	D	T
Y	N	D	E	P	T	R	A	C
T	P	C	A	D	R	N	Y	E
N	Y	P	R	C	D	E	T	A
C	T	E	N	Y	A	D	R	P
D	R	A	T	E	P	Y	C	N
A	C	N	D	R	E	T	P	Y
P	D	Y	C	T	N	A	E	R
R	E	T	P	A	Y	C	N	D

PUZZLE 35

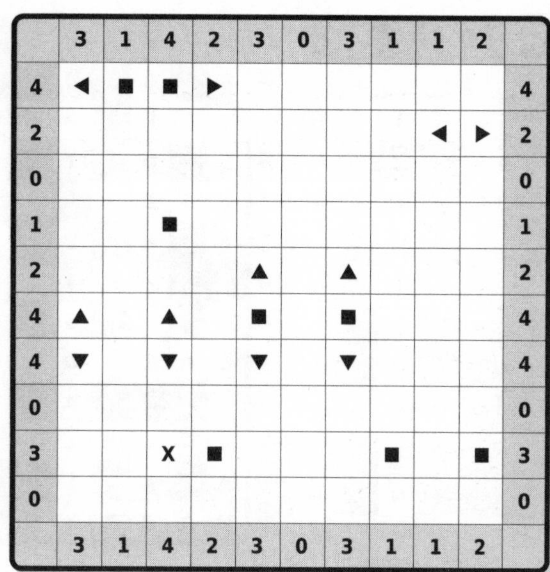

PUZZLE 36

Condemn Russia, Serbia and France. Condemning Russia will soothe Bulgaria's anger and make Germany happy, but put you in the bad books of Austria-Hungary and Romania. Condemning Serbia will put things right with Austria-Hungary and make Bulgaria even happier, and it will make Germany neutral and anger the Ottomans. Condemning France will put things right with Romania and the Ottoman Empire.

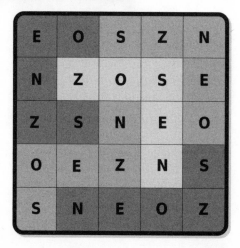

PUZZLE 37

E	O	S	Z	N
N	Z	O	S	E
Z	S	N	E	O
O	E	Z	N	S
S	N	E	O	Z

PUZZLE 38

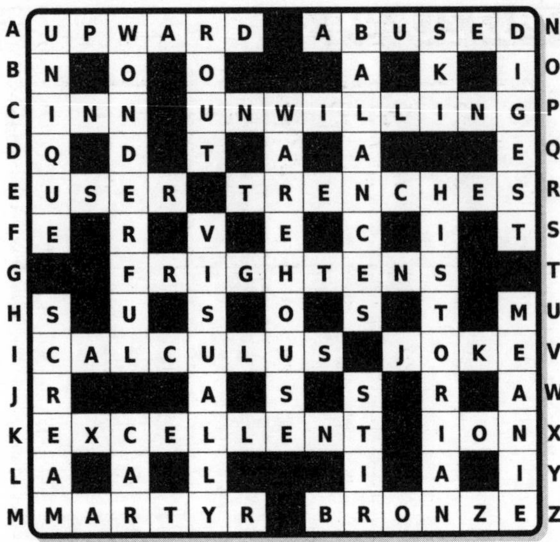

1	2	3	4	5	6	7	8	9	10	11	12	13
B	D	Y	A	W	H	V	F	K	C	G	N	L
14	15	16	17	18	19	20	21	22	23	24	25	26
J	O	Q	Z	S	R	X	E	I	U	P	T	M

PUZZLE 39

▬ ▬ • •

E eins
Z zwei
D drei
V vier

F fünf
S sechs
S sieben
A acht

N neun
Z zehn
E elf
Z zwölf

Alfred von Schlieffen was a German count – and so is this puzzle!

PUZZLE 40

Z	R	N	E	L	D	S	P	I
S	E	L	I	Z	P	R	D	N
I	D	P	N	S	R	Z	E	L
E	S	R	P	I	N	L	Z	D
L	N	D	S	E	Z	P	I	R
P	I	Z	D	R	L	N	S	E
D	Z	E	R	N	S	I	L	P
R	P	S	L	D	I	E	N	Z
N	L	I	Z	P	E	D	R	S

PUZZLE 41

Yesterday our cryptology department decrypted this message and we can confirm that the letter R occurs **fourteen** times. No further action is required.

PUZZLE 42

Keyword: A Balkan country that yearns to be free: **BOSNIA**

I am a Yugoslav nationalist, aiming for the unification of all Yugoslavs, and I do not care what form of state, but it must be freed from Austria.

This is a quote from Gavrilo Princip at his trial.

PUZZLE 43

The picture reveals **MORSE CODE,** with the word 'code' further encrypted in Morse code itself (read vertically).

	5	4					5		4		5	3	2	
4					6	4		4		5	8	5		
3	6	3		3		3	6		6			4		
			6	3		4	7	4		5				0
		2							4				1	
3		3	4		5	4	5			2	4	2		1
3				3			3			2	4			
5	7	4			6					2		2		1
				4	4	1	2				4			
4	7			5			2	1	3	2			1	
			4		4	2	3			2				
	3		2			2		2	4				1	
	0						2	2			3			
					0			2			2			
	0			0			1		2				0	

PUZZLE 44

CLUE: The longest word is the capital of the Ottoman Empire: **CONSTANTINOPLE.**

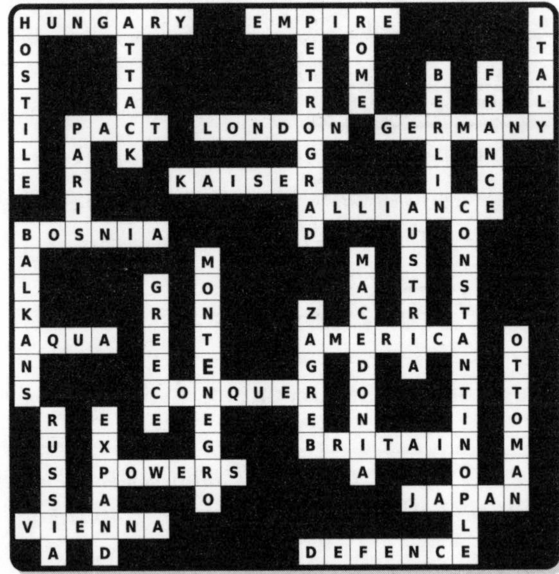

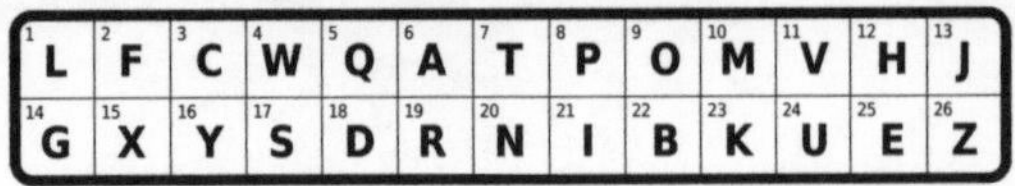

1	2	3	4	5	6	7	8	9	10	11	12	13
L	F	C	W	Q	A	T	P	O	M	V	H	J
14	**15**	**16**	**17**	**18**	**19**	**20**	**21**	**22**	**23**	**24**	**25**	**26**
G	X	Y	S	D	R	N	I	B	K	U	E	Z

PUZZLE 45

CLUE: Vigenère Cipher / CHURCHILL

the most insolent document of its kind ever devised

PUZZLE 46

Certainly not! He doesn't like the letter 'R'.

PUZZLE 47

Five storeys. The top storey is two cards, and each storey contains three more cards than the one above it. A five-storey house would consist of 40 cards, while six storeys would require 57.

PUZZLE 48

Number 5. First you must decrypt each line with a Caesar shift – the number before each sentence is its key.

1. all of those below are true
2. none of those below are true
3. one of those above is true
4. all of those above are true
5. none of those above is true
6. all of those above are false

Since 2 and 4 cannot both be true, 1 must be false.

3 must be false because if it were true, it would make 2 true, which is self-contradicting.

4 is false because we now know that 1 and 3 refute it.

2 cannot be true because to confirm it 6 would have to be true, which makes 2 false.

5 is therefore true.

6 cannot be true because 5 is true, which makes 6 false.

PUZZLE 49

1. **Allied:** Hidden behind a wall, I edged closer to the enemy.
2. **Axis:** The morning briefing was an anticlimax; I sensed they had run out of ideas.
3. **Treaty:** I saw, flying towards the town centre, a type of aircraft I'd never seen before.
4. **Armistice:** Weather conditions felt almost polar; mist, ice and blizzards made for very cold nights on the Western Front.
5. **Morale:** A hot meal could help to break the tedium, or a letter from home – that was very special indeed.

PUZZLE 50

Yes, Henry is 20 years old. If Henry's age is x, then Mark's age is x/2 and his father's age is 2x. So, in 20 years Mark's age will be x/2 +20 and his father will be 2x+20. As Mark will be half his father's age:

$2(x/2 +20) = 2x+20.$
$x+40 = 2x+20.$
$x = 20.$

PUZZLE 51

Did you consider solving the puzzle in three dimensions?

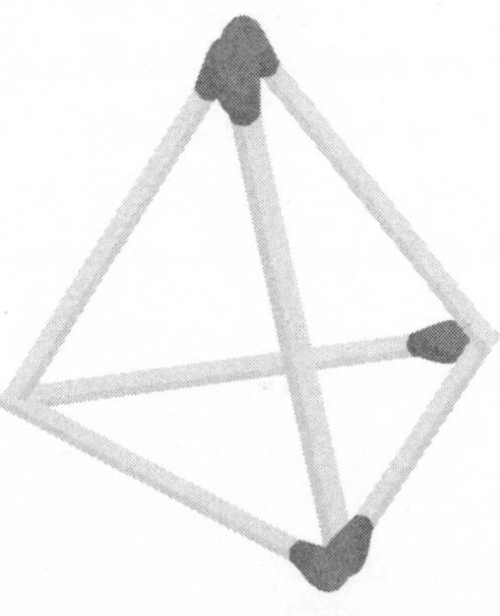

PUZZLE 52

Multiply the digits of each number to get the next number.

77	49	36	18	8
	7 x 7	4 x 9	3 x 6	1 x 8

PUZZLE 53

	2	●	2	●			1	
●		2		1	1	1	●	
2	●	3	2			2		2
2		●	●	1		●	3	●
●	4		3		2	●	4	
●	3	●		1			●	2
1		1		●	1	3	●	3
		2	3	2		3	●	
●	2	●	●		1	●	3	●

PUZZLE 54

Previously, many of the soldiers who sustained a head injury from a bullet or shrapnel would have died before reaching the hospital.

PUZZLE 55

CLUE: Poetry (keyword). 'The Kiss', a poem written by Siegfried Sassoon in 1916.

To these I turn, in these I trust–
Brother Lead and Sister Steel.
To his blind power I make appeal,
I guard her beauty clean from rust.

He spins and burns and loves the air,
And splits a skull to win my praise;
But up the nobly marching days
She glitters naked, cold and fair.

Sweet Sister, grant your soldier this:
That in good fury he may feel
The body where he sets his heel
Quail from your downward darting kiss.

PUZZLE 56

East

B	D	C	D	B	D	A	D	A	B	C	B
A	C	B	A	D	C	B	C	D	A	D	A
A	B	A	D	C	B	D	B	A	B	C	A
B	C	D	B	D	A	D	B	D	C	D	B
C	D	A	D	C	B	A	D	A	B	C	A
A	B	C	A	D	C	D	B	D	C	B	C
D	A	B	D	C	D	C	A	C	D	A	D
B	C	D	A	B	A	B	C	D	A	B	A
C	A	A	C	D	A	C	A	C	D	A	B

West

PUZZLE 57

They can dig **60 metres** of trench.

6 French can dig 6 metres in 6 hours, so
12 French can dig 12 metres in 6 hours and
12 French can dig **24 metres** in 12 hours.
4 British can dig 4 metres in 4 hours, so
12 British can dig 12 metres in 4 hours and
12 British can dig **36 metres** in 12 hours.

PUZZLE 58

The hidden word was ALLIANCE.

A		R		G		C		A		U		E		N
B	R	E	V	E	A	L		L	I	N	I	N	G	O
C		S		N		I		K		S		T		P
D	S	I	Z	E		Q	U	A	R	T	E	R	S	Q
E		D				U		L		E		Y		R
F	H	E	X	A	D	E	C	I	M	A	L			S
G		S		L						D		I		T
H			C	L	A	S	S	I	F	Y	I	N	G	U
I		B		I		E		N				J		V
J	G	L	E	A	N	I	N	G		B	L	U	R	W
K		I		N		Z		E		I		R		X
L	P	S	Y	C	H	E		S	H	O	W	E	D	Y
M		S		E		D		T		S		S		Z

1	2	3	4	5	6	7	8	9	10	11	12	13
S	B	W	O	Z	H	N	U	L	V	X	G	K

14	15	16	17	18	19	20	21	22	23	24	25	26
J	D	E	M	A	I	R	T	Q	C	F	Y	P

PUZZLE 59

The key is **TANKS**. The message has been encrypted with a columnar transposition cipher.

T	A	N	K	S
F	R	O	M	W
H	E	R	E	D
O	E	S	T	H
E	T	A	N	K
G	E	T	I	T
S	N	A	M	E

Q: From where does the tank get its name?

A: It was a code name concocted by the British so the Germans would think the vehicles were water carriers headed for battle in the Middle East.

PUZZLE 60

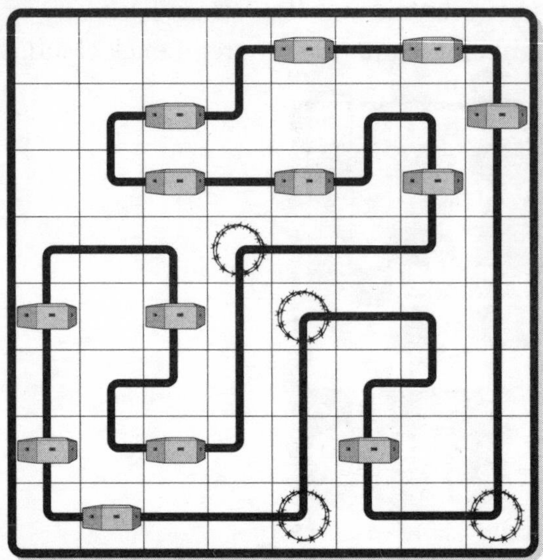

PUZZLE 61

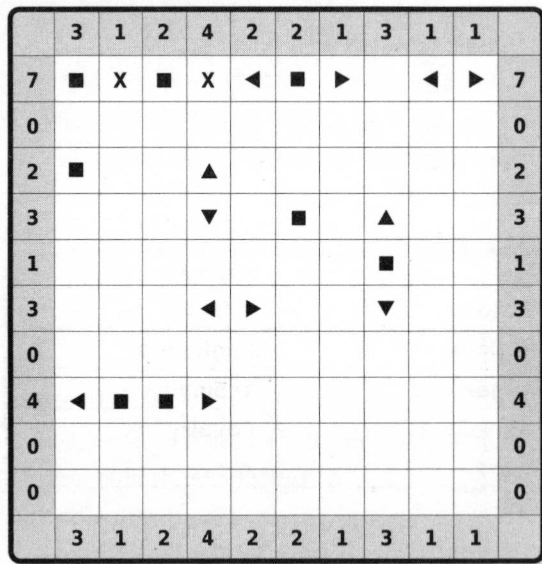

	3	1	2	4	2	2	1	3	1	1	
7	■	X	■	X	◀	■	▶		◀	▶	7
0											0
2	■			▲							2
3				▼		■		▲			3
1								■			1
3				◀	▶			▼			3
0											0
4	◀	■	■	▶							4
0											0
0											0
	3	1	2	4	2	2	1	3	1	1	

PUZZLE 62

B. Each row and each column contain two fighters and one airship, two squares of light cloud and one square of thick cloud.

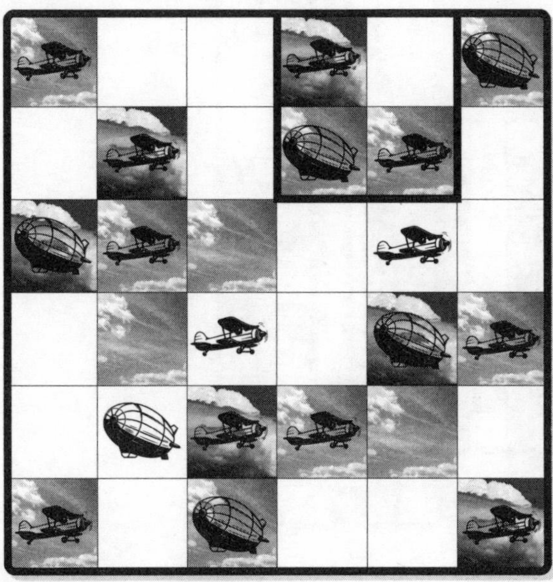

PUZZLE 63

22 times. They meet every $1\,^{1}/_{11}$ hour.

PUZZLE 64

Surname	Rank	Regiment
Jones	**Private**	**Infantry**
Smith	**Corporal**	**Engineers**
Webster	**Sergeant**	**Yeomanry**
Anderson	**Lieutenant**	**Cavalry**
Barnes	**Major**	**Artillery**

PUZZLE 65

The picture reveals **NO MAN'S LAND.**

3	5	3			5	3	2							0		
4				4						0		0				0
	6	3				4	3					1	1	1		
	4	2			5								1		0	
3			4							2	3	3			3	
		3	4		4		5	3	4			3	4		4	
4				4		5		5		4					7	
3			5	3			7	4					5	3		
	4	1	4						6			3				
2	2			2	4		4	2		2			3	2	4	3
	2			3	5									3	3	
		0	2			3			5		4	3	4	2	1	
	3		3		8	5	6				6			3	2	
	5	2				4		3						3		
	4				5		4	2		2		3	4	2	1	

PUZZLE 66

A	E	L	T	R	M	S	I	C
S	R	I	A	C	E	T	L	M
C	T	M	L	I	S	E	R	A
M	A	R	I	E	L	C	T	S
T	I	C	R	S	A	M	E	L
L	S	E	C	M	T	R	A	I
E	L	A	S	T	C	I	M	R
I	M	S	E	A	R	L	C	T
R	C	T	M	L	I	A	S	E

PUZZLE 67

Working from both ends of the number line, the highest and lowest numbers have a sum of 101.

1 + 100 = 101, 2 + 99 = 101, 3 + 98 = 101… until 50 + 51 = 101.

So, the answer is 50 x 101 = 5050.

PUZZLE 68

								R	A	D	A	R
						F				U		E
S	P	I	T	F	I	R	E			N		T
				I		A				K		R
A		M	A	G	I	N	O	T	L	I	N	E
R		A		H		C				R		A
M	U	N	I	T	I	O	N	S		K		T
I		C		E				E				
S		H	U	R	R	I	C	A	N	E		A
T		U		S				L				N
I		R			C	I	V	I	L	I	A	N
C		I						O				E
E		A	B	Y	S	S	I	N	I	A		X

PUZZLE 69

The Morse sequence is the elements with atomic numbers 5 to 9 from the periodic table.

B = Boron, **C** = Carbon, **N** = Nitrogen, **O** = Oxygen and **F** = Fluorine.

PUZZLE 70

1. Benito Mussolini
2. Dwight D. Eisenhower
3. Joseph Stalin
4. Charles de Gaulle
5. Douglas Bader
6. Vera Lynn
7. Hugh Dowding
8. Erwin Rommel

PUZZLE 71

R	L	E	A	I	H	D	S	N
N	H	D	E	R	S	I	A	L
A	S	I	L	N	D	R	H	E
L	D	R	N	S	A	H	E	I
H	A	S	D	E	I	N	L	R
I	E	N	R	H	L	S	D	A
D	N	H	I	L	E	A	R	S
E	I	A	S	D	R	L	N	H
S	R	L	H	A	N	E	I	D

PUZZLE 72

The hidden ideology was **COMMUNISM**.

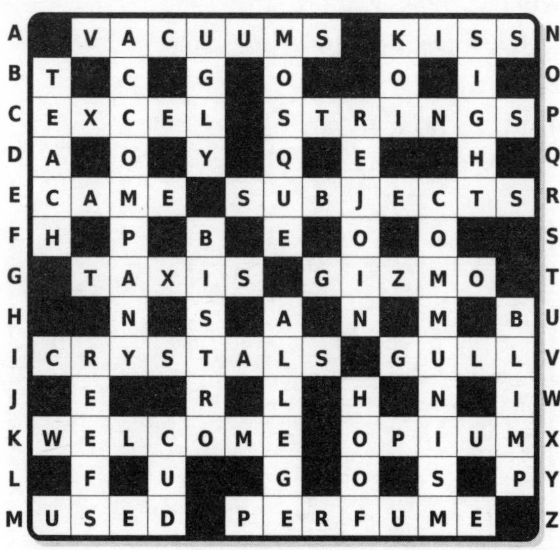

1	2	3	4	5	6	7	8	9	10	11	12	13
H	Z	N	F	Q	X	L	U	D	W	P	K	S
14	**15**	**16**	**17**	**18**	**19**	**20**	**21**	**22**	**23**	**24**	**25**	**26**
E	O	R	C	B	I	V	G	M	J	Y	A	T

PUZZLE 73

The letters combined are anagrams.

1. Franklin D. Roosevelt **CAMILA**
2. Charles de Gaulle **FANNIE**
3. Joseph Stalin **DEBORA**
4. Benito Mussolini **AGATHA**
5. Hermann Göring **GINGER**
6. Winston Churchill **BRENDA**

PUZZLE 74

Operation Konserve or Operation 'Canned Goods'. It was encrypted with Caesar Shift 12. Did you quickly deduce that the first word was 'Operation' to save time?

PUZZLE 75

1: A V-1 flying bomb.

2: The annexation of Austria by Nazi Germany.

3: Modified tanks used for special engineering tasks.

4: Rural French Resistance fighters.

5: The German word for the Phoney War (3 September 1939 – 10 May 1940).

PUZZLE 76

	3	1	3	1	3	1	3	1	2	2	
3							▲		◀	▶	3
5	◀	■	■	▶			▼				5
0											0
1					▲						1
3	■		■		■						3
1					▼						1
2	■		■								2
3						◀	■	▶			3
0											0
2									◀	▶	2
	3	1	3	1	3	1	3	1	2	2	

PUZZLE 77

The unscrambled names are, in order:

Truman + A
Churchill + L
Roosevelt + L
Stalin + I
Chamberlain + E
De Gaulle + D

The additional letters spell '**ALLIED**'.

PUZZLE 78

44 motorbikes

If motorbikes are x and cars are y

$x + y = 72$ (vehicles)

$2x + 4y = 200$ (wheels)

So, $x + 2y = 100$

$y = 28$ and $x = 44$.

PUZZLE 79

2	2	2		1		●
	●●		2	●	3	2
2		3	●	4	●	
	2			4	●	2
2	●●	5	●	2	3	3
4		●●	6			●●
●●	6	●●	5	●	3	2

PUZZLE 80

JOSEPH STALIN.

ARGON	+J JARGON	NEW	+S NEWS
SOON	-O SON	TRUST	-T RUST
TEAM	+S STEAM	RID	+A RAID
EMOTION	-E MOTION	LAIR	-L AIR
STRIPPED	-P STRIPED	COINED	-I CONED
LATER	+H LATHER	LACE	+N LANCE

PUZZLE 81

1. **Radar**: The troops in Stalingrad are determined not to surrender.

2. **Spitfire**: The army had victory in its grasp; it fired relentlessly at the enemy lines.

3. **Panzer**: Japan zeroed in on Pearl Harbor as a target later in the war.

4. **Sonar**: Success depends on a replenished air force.

5. **Sherman**: The intelligence officer still needs her mandatory field training.

PUZZLE 82

The quotes were all encrypted with Atbash.

4 'I have nothing to offer but blood, toil, tears and sweat.'

13 May 1940

2 '…we shall fight in the hills; we shall never surrender.'

4 June 1940

1 '…men will still say, "This was their finest hour"…'

18 June 1940

3 'Never in the field of human conflict was so much owed by so many to so few.'

20 August 1940

PUZZLE 83

The hidden method of diplomacy was **APPEASEMENT**.

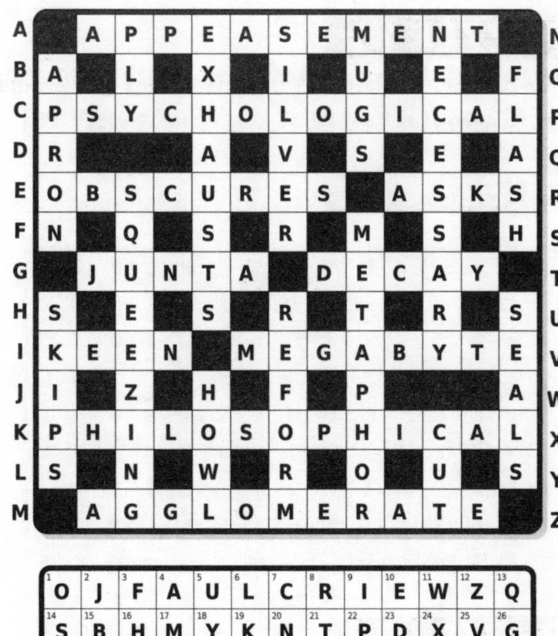

PUZZLE 84

Half an hour. Clocks in the 1940s were mechanical and did not differentiate between am and pm.

PUZZLE 85

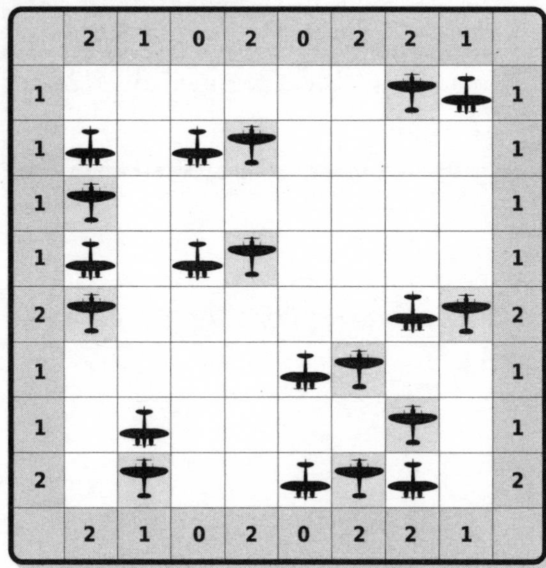

PUZZLE 86

9, 2 and 2. There are two possibilities. By stating that the eldest child was not a twin, it ruled out the other (1, 6 and 6).

PUZZLE 87

K	N	Y	H	T	U	O	M	S	T	R	O	P	C	R
L	C	O	P	I	L	Y	W	X	M	M	I	Q	M	B
I	W	W	G	L	Y	T	S	A	F	L	E	B	R	U
V	L	B	U	A	E	S	N	A	W	S	Q	I	Q	D
E	V	H	B	Y	Q	C	U	Y	Z	X	S	B	N	L
R	Y	S	E	I	H	G	C	Q	F	T	P	O	S	E
P	F	A	V	E	L	R	P	J	O	L	T	T	X	I
O	P	G	S	A	M	F	L	L	Y	P	J	Y	O	F
O	E	T	S	C	F	L	U	M	M	Q	Q	R	C	F
L	E	G	L	I	H	P	O	A	H	B	B	T	A	E
R	O	V	D	W	D	U	H	N	A	U	O	N	L	H
W	Y	R	M	G	T	T	K	L	D	R	P	E	Z	S
H	A	H	N	H	U	H	Z	X	G	O	H	V	L	B
C	S	K	U	O	G	A	O	I	T	S	N	O	H	L
A	S	L	S	G	P	I	Y	K	V	I	I	C	I	S

BELFAST
BRISTOL
CARDIFF
COVENTRY
GLASGOW
HULL
LIVERPOOL
LONDON
MANCHESTER
PLYMOUTH
PORTSMOUTH
SHEFFIELD
SOUTHAMPTON
SWANSEA

PUZZLE 88

Agent	Code Name	Location	Network
Odette	*Lise*	Annecy	Spindle
Nora	*Madeleine*	Paris	Cinema
Yvonne	*Annette*	Bordeaux	Wheelwright

PUZZLE 89

1. 60. For the first rotor slot there are 5 options, for the second 4 and for the third 3. (5 x 4 x 3)

2. 17,576 (26 x 26 x 26)

PUZZLE 90

'The geese that laid the golden eggs (but never cackled)'

This was a quote from Winston Churchill, admiring the invaluable work of the Bletchley Park codebreakers and how they kept it a secret.

The key is **GANDER** and the message has been encrypted with a columnar transposition cipher. Clue: British slang for a glance.

G	A	N	D	E	R
T	H	E	G	E	E
S	E	T	H	A	T
L	A	I	D	T	H
E	G	O	L	D	E
N	E	G	G	S	X

PUZZLE 91

'C'. The first director signed his letters in green ink with a 'C' for Cumming. The fictional character 'M' in the James Bond stories was Ian Fleming's nod to the tradition.

PUZZLE 92

The hidden military tactic was **BLITZKRIEG**.

A			A		P		S		S		A			N
B	U	D	D	E	R		P	U	P	I	L	S		O
C	N		J		O		A		E		G		B	P
D	O	P	A	Q	U	E	R		C	R	A	W	L	Q
E	F		C		D		E		I				I	R
F	F	L	E	X		W		E	F	F	E	C	T	S
G	I		N		F	A	I	R	Y		M		Z	T
H	C	I	T	R	U	S		R		T	U	C	K	U
I	I				R		C		R		L		R	V
J	A	W	A	I	T		O	R	I	G	A	M	I	W
K	L		M		H		Y		V		T		E	X
L		U	P	K	E	E	P		A	L	O	N	G	Y
M			S		R		U		L		R			Z

1	2	3	4	5	6	7	8	9	10	11	12	13
G	J	O	K	Z	C	F	T	N	Q	X	S	E

14	15	16	17	18	19	20	21	22	23	24	25	26
H	D	M	B	L	A	R	Y	U	P	I	V	W

PUZZLE 93

'The battle beginning today will decide the fate of the German nation for the next thousand years.' A quote from Adolf Hitler, 10 May 1940.

STEP 1

Plaintext												
a	**b**	**c**	**d**	**e**	**f**	**g**	**h**	**i**	**j**	**k**	**l**	**m**
M	Z	C	N	K	F	W	P	Y	J	E	V	A
Ciphertext												
Plaintext												
n	**o**	**p**	**q**	**r**	**s**	**t**	**u**	**v**	**w**	**x**	**y**	**z**
D	S	H	Q	T	O	R	U	L	G	X	I	B
Ciphertext												

THE QUICK BROWN FOX JUMPED OVER THE LAZY DOG

So, your second stage ciphertext becomes:

EQTWUBBJNQNLGBBGYFSXFIKMXUUC
YAUZVGSVRWDSFOAMMKMZBNAA
KRCWUCTQLXARXEIIRKEGVISXOSBA

STEP 2

START: 2 El Alamein 1942
LENGTH: 4 Monte Cassino 1944
INCREMENT: 3 Kursk 1943

PUZZLE 94

The Morse dots and dashes are anagrams.

SALINE = HHO (H2O, water) + **NACL** (sodium chloride, salt)

PUZZLE 95

2D	2R	2L	1D
2R	2D	3D	2L
2D	1R	**OPEN**	2L
2R	1L	3U	1U
3R	4U	1L	1U

PUZZLE 96

		●	2	1			●	2
●	3			●		●	4	●
3	●	2	1		3	●	3	
	●				2			
2		3	●	●		1	●	●
2	●	3			2			3
	●	3	2	●			3	●
2	3	●	3		2	2	●	●
●		2	●	1		●	3	2

PUZZLE 97

1. **Keypress**: We need to make Ypres seem like the target of the operation.

2. **Ultra**: We think the consul tracked us to this location.

3. **Rotor**: The operation went from zero to roaring success in less than a week.

4. **Turing**: We found a crucial non sequitur in German intelligence transcripts.

5. **Boniface**: The machine turns a light bulb on if a certain letter is encrypted.

PUZZLE 98

V	T	M	U	M	D	R	C	Z	F	Q	X	Y	S	X
I	S	O	S	C	I	E	N	T	I	S	T	G	M	H
Q	I	Y	J	L	Q	F	J	D	W	M	M	C	P	G
E	U	O	P	T	H	O	O	Z	A	G	G	H	T	H
P	Q	T	H	H	C	Q	I	R	Y	E	E	A	E	G
F	O	K	K	K	O	K	K	K	V	W	B	A	N	P
R	L	V	E	Q	U	S	D	I	C	O	D	U	R	H
E	I	Y	D	I	M	N	T	R	R	M	R	K	E	Y
E	R	D	W	A	R	C	D	C	A	C	X	N	K	S
L	T	T	N	B	E	L	A	S	H	Z	I	O	N	I
A	N	V	Z	T	T	J	T	I	N	O	I	M	I	C
N	E	V	E	A	M	E	N	I	C	J	D	W	T	I
C	V	D	Z	G	R	H	L	Y	J	H	Z	G	V	A
E	H	G	P	B	R	I	C	K	L	A	Y	E	R	N
L	T	C	H	W	N	N	H	F	W	D	C	J	D	E

ACROBAT
BRICKLAYER
CINEMA
DETECTIVE
FREELANCE
HEADMASTER
JOCKEY
MARKSMAN
MONK
PHYSICIAN
SCIENTIST
TINKER
URCHIN
VENTRILOQUIST
WIZARD

PUZZLE 99

Initially the **SOE** operated out of an inconspicuous flat at **64 BAKER STREET**, London, which inevitably connected it to England's greatest fictional detective. **SHERLOCK** is the key to this keyword cipher.

PUZZLE 100

Yes, he is five times better. The value of each name is its first letter as a Roman numeral.

PUZZLE 101

'A date which will live in infamy.'

President Roosevelt's response to the attack on Pearl Harbor. It was encrypted with the Vigenère cipher using the keyword **SAKE**.

PUZZLE 102

	0	6	0	2	3	1	1	2	5	0	
0											0
2		▲			■						2
3		■						◀	▶		3
2		■			■						2
3		▼						◀	▶		3
0											0
3					◀	■	▶				3
2		■							▲		2
2				▲					■		2
3		■		▼					▼		3
	0	6	0	2	3	1	1	2	5	0	

PUZZLE 103

ENVELOPE!

PUZZLE 104

'Now this is not the end. It is not even the beginning of the end. But it is, perhaps, the end of the beginning.'

This was from Winston Churchill's famous speech on 10 November 1942 following victory at El Alamein.

It was encrypted with the Alberti Cipher, **start:** 3; **length:** 2; **increment:** 1.

PUZZLE 105

It was a cloud of aluminium strips released from the aircraft to confuse enemy radar.

PUZZLE 106

This rather cynical blueprint for how Eastern Europe might be divided between Britain and Russia after the war was referred to as the '**NAUGHTY**' document by Churchill. **NAUGHTY** is the key to this keyword cipher and the numbers are percentages.

	RUSSIA	BRITAIN
ROMANIA	90	10
GREECE	90	10
YUGOSLAVIA	50	50
HUNGARY	50	50
BULGARIA	75	25

PUZZLE 107

The picture reveals a series of Morse code letters spelling **RESISTANCE**.

			2		1	1	0			1
2	4	3		3		1		2		
1		1	2	1	1	0	1	1	2	1
2	4	2			2	0	2	3	4	2
	2		2	1	1		1		2	1
	4		4	2	1		3			2
1	2	2		1			2	2	2	
3	4		3	3		3			3	1
2	2	2	1			2	2		1	
			1		2	2	2	1	1	
1	1	0								

PUZZLE 108

The operational words are **MARKET GARDEN**.

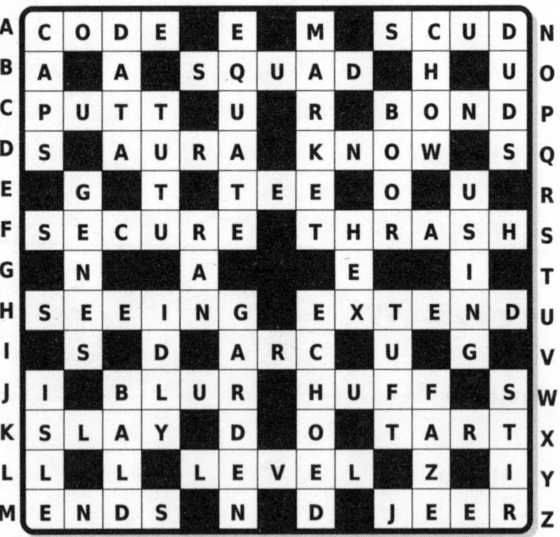

1	2	3	4	5	6	7	8	9	10	11	12	13
U	A	D	M	H	J	W	V	S	B	E	O	Y
14	**15**	**16**	**17**	**18**	**19**	**20**	**21**	**22**	**23**	**24**	**25**	**26**
K	C	Z	R	P	N	Q	G	X	F	T	L	I

PUZZLE 109

The unscrambled operation names are, in order:

Market Garden	**+ I**
Plunder	**+ N**
Lena	**+ V**
Iceberg	**+ A**
Mincemeat	**+ S**
Overlord	**+ I**
Varsity	**+ O**
Barbarossa	**+ N**

The additional letters spell '**INVASION**'.

PUZZLE 110

D	D	A	Y					B				
I		N		R		B		A			L	
P		T		H		O		R	O	T	O	R
L		W		I		D		B			R	
O		E		N		Y		A			E	
M	A	R	K	E	T	G	A	R	D	E	N	
A		P				U		O			Z	
T			L	E	N	A		S	I	S		P
		U		N		R		S		W		A
J		L		I		D	R	A	G	O	O	N
U		T		G						R		Z
N		R		M			G	O	L	D		E
O	M	A	H	A								R

PUZZLE 111

This Sudoku has been encrypted with the letters **AHILMORST**. Solve it to find the word revealed in the shaded boxes.

H	O	L	R	T	I	S	A	M
T	I	M	S	O	A	L	R	H
S	A	R	H	M	L	T	O	I
I	L	A	O	R	T	M	H	S
O	H	T	I	S	M	A	L	R
R	M	S	A	L	H	O	I	T
L	R	H	M	A	S	I	T	O
A	S	O	T	I	R	H	M	L
M	T	I	L	H	O	R	S	A

PUZZLE 112

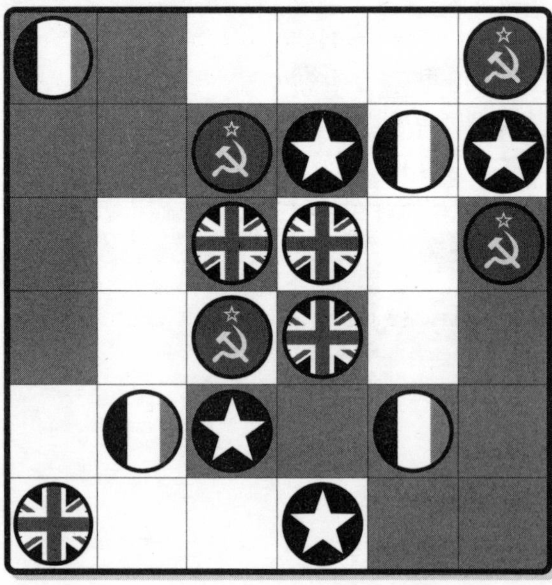

PUZZLE 113

The hidden Western policy was **CONTAINMENT**.

1	2	3	4	5	6	7	8	9	10	11	12	13
J	Y	B	O	E	H	L	P	N	V	G	F	R
14	**15**	**16**	**17**	**18**	**19**	**20**	**21**	**22**	**23**	**24**	**25**	**26**
D	W	U	Z	K	A	T	Q	X	M	S	C	I

PUZZLE 114

'It must be the policy of the United States to support free peoples who are resisting attempted subjugation by armed minorities or by outside pressures.'

Harry S. Truman, outlining his doctrine to Congress on 12 March 1947.

The clue was 'Independence Day' (4 July). The text was encrypted with Caesar Shift 4.

PUZZLE 115

●	2			●	3	●		1	2	●
2	●	2		4	●	4			●	4
			●	●	3	●	●		●	●
1		2	4	4				3	●	4
●	1		●	●	2		2		4	●
1		2		4	●	2	●	●		●
		●	3	●	3	4		4		●
●	●	●		3	●		●	●	3	2
	4		2	●	3		2		3	●
2	●		2		●	1		3	●	4
	●	3	●				1	●	●	●

PUZZLE 116

'From Stettin in the Baltic to Trieste in the Adriatic, an iron curtain has descended across the continent.'

Former Prime Minister Winston Churchill, from a speech at Westminster College, Missouri in 1946.

The text was encrypted with a keyword cipher (RINGO) obtained from the clue JOHNPAULGEORGE.

PUZZLE 117

B	O	I	G	S	A	Y	P	F
S	A	G	P	Y	F	B	O	I
F	P	Y	B	O	I	S	A	G
A	S	F	O	B	Y	G	I	P
O	I	P	S	F	G	A	Y	B
Y	G	B	I	A	P	F	S	O
P	Y	O	F	G	S	I	B	A
I	F	S	A	P	B	O	G	Y
G	B	A	Y	I	O	P	F	S

PUZZLE 118

The hidden combatants were **SUPERPOWERS**.

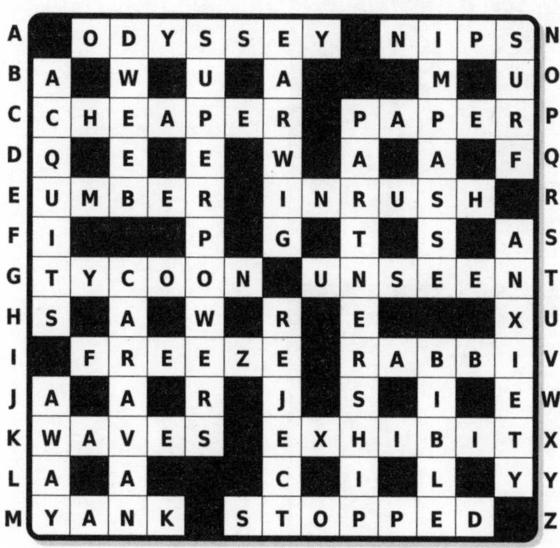

PUZZLE 119

The unscrambled country names, in order, are:

Belgium	+	**A**
United States	+	**T**
United Kingdom	+	**L**
Portugal	+	**A**
Norway	+	**N**
Netherlands	+	**T**
Denmark	+	**I**
Iceland	+	**C**

The additional letters spell '**ATLANTIC**'. All of the countries were signatories to the North Atlantic Treaty, forming NATO (along with other countries).

PUZZLE 120

The hidden text is **SOVIET**.

	4	2				3	4			
5		4			7			3		3
3	5		5	3	6	3	6	3		3
	7		6		7		5		5	
		3			5					
4								3		
	4	3		3	4		2			3
	5		4		6	3	2	4	5	
	3	3			4				3	
			4					3	3	3
	4				4	2				

PUZZLE 121

1. **Missile:** The control room is silent before a mission commences.
2. **Orbit:** The technical director bitterly regretted his team's failures.
3. **Apollo:** A poll – or popular vote – will be held to name the new department.
4. **Satellite:** With spies, there's always a tell; I tend to spot traitors a mile off.
5. **NASA:** That event will always be seen as a technological miracle.

PUZZLE 122

All three men saved the world. Clark Kent (as Superman) saved Earth multiple times, most notably from the villainous Lex Luthor. Vasili Arkhipov was an officer in the Soviet Navy who refused to authorize the use of a submarine's nuclear torpedoes against the US Navy during the Cuban Missile Crisis – his courage and good judgement are widely believed to have saved the world from a thermonuclear war. Stanislav Petrov was a Soviet Union Air Defence Forces lieutenant colonel who disobeyed an order to launch a retaliatory nuclear strike against the USA in 1983; he rightly judged that reports of an incoming US attack were false. Clark Kent is fictional.

PUZZLE 123

The new danger was **THERMONUCLEAR.**

A	P	U	B	L	I	C		T	I	P	T	O	E	N
B		N		A		O		H		R		N		O
C	Q	U	A	D		M	N	E	M	O	N	I	C	P
D		S		L		P		R		J		O		Q
E	L	U	K	E	W	A	R	M		E	O	N	S	R
F		A				T		O		C				S
G	A	L	K	A	L	I		N	O	T	I	F	Y	T
H				B		B		U				I		U
I	T	O	F	U		I	N	C	O	M	I	N	G	V
J		R		S		L		L		A		D		W
K	M	A	X	I	M	I	Z	E		L	O	I	N	X
L		T		V		T		A		E		N		Y
M	R	E	M	E	D	Y		R	E	S	I	G	N	Z

1	2	3	4	5	6	7	8	9	10	11	12	13
I	N	S	J	P	M	Q	W	G	T	F	H	A
14	**15**	**16**	**17**	**18**	**19**	**20**	**21**	**22**	**23**	**24**	**25**	**26**
O	Z	R	E	Y	X	C	U	B	V	D	K	L

PUZZLE 124

S	I	C	N	L	E	M	T	A
E	T	N	M	C	A	S	I	L
M	L	A	S	T	I	N	E	C
N	A	T	L	M	S	E	C	I
C	S	E	A	I	T	L	M	N
I	M	L	C	E	N	T	A	S
L	E	S	T	A	C	I	N	M
T	C	M	I	N	L	A	S	E
A	N	I	E	S	M	C	L	T

PUZZLE 125

The dangerous game was **BRINKMANSHIP**.

A	S	P	R	A	Y		A	B	O	L	I	S	H	N
B		H		F		A		R		E		Q		O
C	C	O	N	F	E	T	T	I		M	A	U	L	P
D		T		A		T		N		M		E		Q
E	R	O	B	B	E	R		K	N	A	V	E		R
F				L		I		M				Z		S
G	R	E	L	Y		B	A	A		B	Y	E	S	T
H		J				U		N		R				U
I		E	X	A	L	T		S	T	O	R	M	S	V
J		C		P		A		H		A		A		W
K	A	T	O	P		B	U	I	L	D	I	N	G	X
L		E		L		L		P		E		G		Y
M	A	D	H	E	R	E	S		A	R	R	O	W	Z

1	2	3	4	5	6	7	8	9	10	11	12	13
X	Y	Z	G	W	H	I	V	D	L	N	A	M
14	**15**	**16**	**17**	**18**	**19**	**20**	**21**	**22**	**23**	**24**	**25**	**26**
T	J	C	R	B	K	E	S	F	U	Q	O	P

PUZZLE 126

PUZZLE 127

1. HARRY S. TRUMAN *(1945 – 1953)*
2. DWIGHT D. EISENHOWER *(1953 – 1961)*
3. JOHN F. KENNEDY *(1961 – 1963)*
4. LYNDON B. JOHNSON *(1963 – 1969)*
5. RICHARD M. NIXON *(1969 – 1974)*
6. GERALD R. FORD *(1974 – 1977)*
7. JAMES E. CARTER *(1977 – 1981)*
8. RONALD W. REAGAN *(1981 – 1989)*
9. GEORGE H.W. BUSH *(1989 – 1993)*